Houghton
Mifflin
Harcourt

GO MATH
Middle School
Grade 6

Practice and Skills
Fluency Workbook

Contents

Student Worksheets

LESSON 1-1

Identifying Integers and Their Opposites

Practice and Problem Solving: A/B

Name a positive or negative number to represent each situation.

1. depositing $85 in a bank account ____

2. riding an elevator down 3 floors ____

3. the foundation of a house sinking 5 inches ____

4. a temperature of 98° above zero ____

Graph each integer and its opposite on the number line.

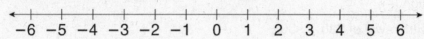

5. –2

6. +3

7. –5

8. +1

Write the correct answers.

9. The average temperature in Fairbanks, Alaska, in February is 4°F below zero. Write this temperature as an integer.

_____

10. The average temperature in Fairbanks, Alaska, in November is 2°F above zero. Write this temperature as an integer.

_____

11. The highest point in the state of Louisiana is Driskill Mountain. It rises 535 feet above sea level. Write the elevation of Driskill Mountain as an integer.

_____

12. The lowest point in the state of Louisiana is New Orleans. The city's elevation is 8 feet below sea level. Write the elevation of New Orleans as an integer.

_____

13. Death Valley, California, has the lowest elevation in the United States. Its elevation is 282 feet below sea level. Mount McKinley, Alaska, has the highest elevation in the United States. Its elevation is 20,320 feet above sea level. Use integers to describe these two locations in the United States.

_____

14. Are there any integers between 0 and 1? Explain.

_____

_____

Name _____ Date _____ Class_____

Identifying Integers and Their Opposites
Reteach

Positive numbers are greater than 0. Use a positive number to represent a gain or increase. Include the positive sign (+).

an increase of 10 points	+10
a flower growth of 2 inches	+2
a gain of 15 yards in football	+15

Negative numbers are less than 0. Use a negative number to represent a loss or decrease. Also use a negative number to represent a value below or less than a certain value. Include the negative sign (–).

a bank withdrawal of $30	–30
a decrease of 9 points	–9
2° below zero	–2

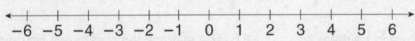

          negative numbers   positive numbers

Opposites are the same distance from zero on the number line, but in different directions. –3 and 3 are opposites because each number is 3 units from zero on a number line.

Integers are the set of all whole numbers, zero, and their opposites.

Name a positive or negative number to represent each situation.

1. an increase of 3 points

2. spending $10

_____

_____

3. earning $25

4. a loss of 5 yards

_____

_____

Write each integer and its opposite. Then graph them on the number line.

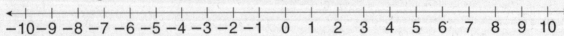

5. –1   6. 9   7. 6   8. –5

_____   _____   _____   _____

Name _____ Date _____ Class_____

Comparing and Ordering Integers
Practice and Problem Solving: A/B

Use the number line to compare each pair of integers. Write < or >.

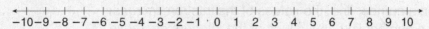

-10 -9 -8 -7 -6 -5 -4 -3 -2 -1 0 1 2 3 4 5 6 7 8 9 10

1. 10 $\bigcirc$ –2

2. 0 $\bigcirc$ 3

3. –5 $\bigcirc$ 0

4. –7 $\bigcirc$ 6

5. –6 $\bigcirc$ –9

6. –8 $\bigcirc$ –10

Order the integers in each set from least to greatest.

7. 5, –2, 6

8. 0, 9, –3,

9. –1, 6, 1

_____   _____   _____

Order the integers in each set from greatest to least.

10. –1, 1, 0

11. –12, 2, 1

12. –10, –12, –11

_____   _____   _____

13. 205, –20, –5, 50

14. –78, –89, 78, 9

15. –55, –2, –60, 0

_____   _____   _____

16. 28, 8, –8, 0

17. 37, –37, –38, 38

18. –111, –1, 1, 11

_____   _____   _____

Solve.

19. Four friends went scuba diving today. Ali dove 70 feet, Tim went down
50 feet, Carl dove 65 feet, and Brenda reached 48 feet below sea
level. Write the 4 friends' names in order from the person whose depth
was closest to the surface to the person whose depth was the farthest
from the surface.

_____

20. Ted is comparing the temperatures of three days in January.
The temperatures on Monday and Tuesday were opposites.
The temperature on Wednesday was neither positive nor negative.
The temperature dropped below zero on Monday. Write the 3 days
in order from the highest to the lowest temperature.

_____

LESSON 1-2

Comparing and Ordering Integers
Reteach

You can use a number line to compare integers.

As you move *right* on a number line, the values of the integers *increase*.
As you move *left* on a number line, the values of the integers *decrease*.

Compare –4 and 2.

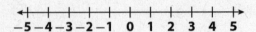

–4 is to the left of 2, so –4 < 2.

Use the number line above to compare the integers. Write < or >.

1. 1 ◯ –4   2. –5 ◯ –2   3. –3 ◯ 2

4. –1 ◯ –4   5. 5 ◯ 0   6. –2 ◯ 3

You can also use a number line to order integers.
Order –3, 4, and –1 from least to greatest.

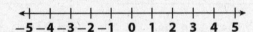

List the numbers in the order in which they appear from left to right.

The integers in order from least to greatest are –3, –1, 4.

Order the integers from least to greatest.

7. –2, –5, –1   8. 0, –5, 5   9. –5, 2, –3

_____   _____   _____

10. 3, –1, –4   11. 3, –5, 0   12. –2, –4, 1

_____   _____   _____

Absolute Value

LESSON 1-3

Practice and Problem Solving: A/B

Graph each number on the number line.

1. −6   2. 3   3. −3   4. 5

Use the number line to find each absolute value.

5. |−6| _____   6. |3| _____   7. |8| _____

8. |6| _____   9. |−3| _____   10. |5| _____

11. What do you notice about the absolute values of 6 and −6?

_____

12. What do you call −6 and 6 or 3 and −3? _____

Use the table for exercises 13–19.

Andrea's Credit-Card Transactions				
Monday	**Tuesday**	**Wednesday**	**Thursday**	**Friday**
Bought $20 shirt	Bought $6 lunch	Made $15 payment	Paid $3 fee	Bought $8 app

Write a negative integer to show the amount spent on each purchase.

13. Monday ____   14. Tuesday ____   15. Friday ____

Find the absolute value of each transaction.

16. Monday ____   17. Tuesday ____   18. Wednesday ____

19. On which day did Andrea spend the most on her card? Explain.

_____

Solve.

20. Show that |3 + 10| = |3| + |10|.

_____

21. How many different integers can have the same absolute

value? _____ Give an example. _____

Absolute Value

LESSON 1-3

Reteach

The absolute value of any number is its distance from 0 on the number line.

Since distance is always positive or 0, absolute value is always positive or 0.

Find the absolute value of −7 and 7.

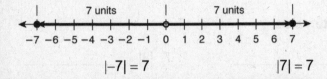

$|-7| = 7$ $|7| = 7$

Match. You can use the letters more than once.

1. absolute value of 15 ____   a. −7

2. negative integer ____   b. 7

3. opposite of −7 ____   c. 15

4. opposite of 7 ____   d. −15

5. |−15| ____

Find each absolute value.

6. |−3| _____   7. |5| _____   8. |−7| _____

9. |6| _____   10. |0| _____   11. |−2| _____

12. |−10| _____   13. $\left|-\dfrac{3}{4}\right|$ _____   14. |0.8| _____

Answer the question.

15. Abby has been absent from class. How would you explain to her what absolute value is? Use the number line and an example in your explanation.

_____

_____

Greatest Common Factor
Practice and Problem Solving: A/B

List the factors of each number.

1. 5

_____

2. 15

_____

3. 60

_____

4. 6

_____

5. 12

_____

6. 36

_____

Find the *greatest common factor* (GCF) for each pair of numbers.

7. 6 and 9

_____

8. 4 and 8

_____

9. 8 and 12

_____

10. 6 and 15

_____

11. 10 and 15

_____

12. 9 and 12

_____

Write the sum of the numbers as the product of their GCF and another sum.

13. $44 + 40 =$

_____

14. $15 + 81 =$

_____

15. $13 + 52 =$

_____

16. $64 + 28 =$

_____

Solve.

17. A jewelry maker will use 24 jade beads and 30 teak beads to make necklaces. Each necklace will have the same numbers of jade beads and teak beads. What is the greatest number of necklaces she can make? How many beads of each type are on each necklace?

_____

18. The marine-life store would like to set up fish tanks that contain equal numbers of angel fish, swordtails, and guppies. What is the greatest number of tanks that can be set up if the store has 12 angel fish, 24 swordtails, and 30 guppies?

_____

Greatest Common Factor

Reteach

The *greatest common factor*, or GCF, is the largest number that is the factor of two or more numbers.

To find the GCF, first write the factors of each number.

Example

Find the GCF of 18 and 24.

Solution Write the factors of 18 and 24. Highlight the *largest* number that is common to both lists of factors.

Factors of 18: 1, 2, 3, **6**, 9, and 18

Factors of 24: 1, 2, 3, 4, **6**, 8, 12, and 24

The GCF of 18 and 24 is 6.

This process works the same way for more than two numbers.

Find the GCF.

1. 32 and 48   2. 18 and 36   3. 28, 56, and 84   4. 30, 45, and 75

_____   _____   _____   _____

The *distributive principle* can be used with the GCF to rewrite a sum of two or more numbers.

Example
Write 30 + 70 as the product of the GCF of 30 and 70 and a sum.

Solution

Step 1 Find the GCF of 30 and 70.

Factors of 30: 1, 2, 3, 5, 6, **10**, 15, and 30

Factors of 70: 1, 2, 5, 7, **10**, 14, 35, and 70. The GCF is 10.

Step 2 Write "10 × (? + ?)." To find the questions marks, divide: 30 ÷ 10 = 3; 70 ÷ 10 = 7

Step 3 So, 30 + 70 can be written as 10 × (3 + 7).

Rewrite each sum as a product of the GCF and a new sum.

5. 9 + 15 =   6. 100 + 350 =   7. 12 + 18 + 21 =

_____   _____   _____

Least Common Multiple

Practice and Problem Solving: A/B

List the first three multiples of each number.

1. 3   2. 7   3. 12   4. 200

_____ _____ _____ _____

Find the *least common multiple* (LCM).

5. 2 and 3   6. 4 and 5   7. 6 and 7

2: _____ 4: _____ 6: _____

3: _____ 5: _____ 7: _____

8. 2, 3, and 4   9. 5, 6, and 7   10. 8, 9, and 10

2: _____ 5: _____ 8: _____

3: _____ 6: _____ 9: _____

4: _____ 7: _____ 10: _____

Solve.

11. Sixty people are invited to a party. There are 24 cups in a package
    and 18 napkins in a package. What is the least number of packages
    of cups and napkins that can be bought if each party guest gets one
    cup and one napkin?

    _____

12. The science club sponsor is ordering caps and shirts for the boys and
    girls in the science club. There are 45 science club members. If the
    caps come in packages of 3 and the shirts come in packages of 5,
    what is the least number of packages of caps and shirts that will need
    to be ordered?

    _____

13. Some hot dogs come in packages of 8. Why would a baker of hot dog
    buns package 7 hot dog buns to a package?

    _____

14. How are the GCF and the LCM alike and different?

    _____

LESSON 2-2

Least Common Multiple

Reteach

The smallest number that is a multiple of two or more numbers is called the least common multiple (LCM) of those numbers.

To find the least common multiple of 3, 6, and 8, list the multiples for each number and put a circle around the LCM in the three lists.

Multiples of 3: 3, 6, 9, 12, 15, 18, 21, 24

Multiples of 6: 6, 12, 18, 24, 30, 36, 42

Multiples of 8: 8, 16, 24, 32, 40, 48, 56

So 24 is the LCM of 3, 6, and 8.

List the multiples of each number to help you find the least common multiple of each group.

1. 2 and 9

   Multiples of 2:

   _____

   Multiples of 9:

   _____

   LCM: _____

2. 4 and 6

   Multiples of 4:

   _____

   Multiples of 6:

   _____

   LCM: _____

3. 4 and 10

   Multiples of 4:

   _____

   Multiples of 10:

   _____

   LCM: _____

4. 2, 5, and 6

   Multiples of 2:

   _____

   Multiples of 5:

   _____

   Multiples of 6:

   _____

   LCM: _____

5. 3, 4, and 9

   Multiples of 3:

   _____

   Multiples of 4:

   _____

   Multiples of 9:

   _____

   LCM: _____

6. 8, 10, and 12

   Multiples of 8:

   _____

   Multiples of 10:

   _____

   Multiples of 12:

   _____

   LCM: _____

7. Pads of paper come 4 to a box, pencils come 27 to a box, and erasers come 12 to a box. What is the least number of kits that can be made with paper, pencils, and erasers with no supplies left over?

   _____

LESSON 3-1 Classifying Rational Numbers

Practice and Problem Solving: A/B

Write each rational number in the form $\frac{a}{b}$, where a and b are integers.

1. 0.3

2. $2\frac{7}{8}$

3. −5

4. 16

_____

_____

_____

_____

5. $-1\frac{3}{4}$

6. −4.5

7. 3

8. 0.11

_____

_____

_____

_____

Place each number in the correct place on the Venn diagram.
Then list all the sets of numbers to which each number belongs.

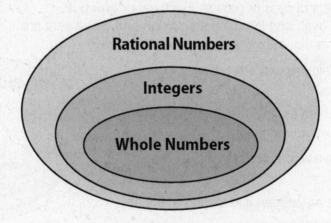

9. −13 _____

10. $\frac{1}{6}$ _____

11. 0 _____

12. 0.99 _____

13. −6.7 _____

14. 34 _____

15. $-14\frac{1}{2}$ _____

LESSON 3-1

Classifying Rational Numbers

Reteach

A rational number is a number that can be written as $\frac{a}{b}$, where a and b are integers and $b \neq 0$. Decimals, fractions, mixed numbers, and integers are all rational numbers.

You can demonstrate a number is rational by writing it in the form $\frac{a}{b}$.

A. $14 = \frac{14}{1}$ Write the whole number over 1.

B. $0.83 = \frac{83}{100}$ Write the decimal as a fraction. Simplify if possible.

C. $5\frac{1}{8} = \frac{41}{8}$ Change the mixed number to an improper fraction.

A Venn diagram is a graphical illustration used to show relationships between various sets of data or groups. Each set or group is represented by an oval, and the relationships among these sets are expressed by their areas of overlap.

- Integers contain the entire set of whole numbers.

- Rational numbers contain the entire sets of integers and whole numbers.

- If a number is a whole number, it is also an integer.

- If a number is an integer, it is to also a rational number.

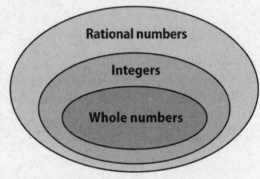

Write each rational number in the form $\frac{a}{b}$, where a and b are integers.

Then circle the name of each set to which the number belongs.

1. −12 _____   Whole Numbers   Integers   Rational Numbers

2. 7.3 _____   Whole Numbers   Integers   Rational Numbers

3. 0.41 _____   Whole Numbers   Integers   Rational Numbers

4. 6 _____   Whole Numbers   Integers   Rational Numbers

5. $3\frac{1}{2}$ _____   Whole Numbers   Integers   Rational Numbers

Identifying Opposites and Absolute Value of Rational Numbers

Practice and Problem Solving: A/B

Graph each number and its opposite on a number line.

1. 3.5

2. –2.5

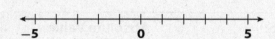   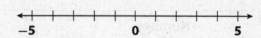

3. $2\dfrac{1}{2}$

4. $-1\dfrac{1}{2}$

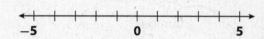

Name the opposite of each number.

5. 4.25 _____

6. $-5\dfrac{1}{4}$ _____

7. $\dfrac{1}{2}$ _____

Name the absolute value of each number.

8. $2\dfrac{1}{3}$ _____

9. –3.85 _____

10. –6.1 _____

**The table shows elevations of checkpoints along a marathon route.
Use the table to answer problems 11–13.**

Checkpoint	A	B	C	D	E
Elevation (ft)	15.6	17.1	5.2	–6.5	–18.5

11. Write the opposite value of each checkpoint elevation.

_____

12. Which checkpoint is closest to sea level? _____

13. Which checkpoint is furthest from sea level? Explain.

_____

_____

Identifying Opposites and Absolute Value of Rational Numbers
Reteach

You can use charts to determine whether the opposites and absolute values of rational numbers are positive or negative.

For positive rational numbers:

Number	Opposite	Absolute Value
3.5	−3.5	3.5
number positive	opposite negative	absolute value always positive

For negative rational numbers:

Number	Opposite	Absolute Value
$-\dfrac{7}{8}$	$\dfrac{7}{8}$	$\dfrac{7}{8}$
number negative	opposite positive	absolute value always positive

Answer each question below.

1. Are the opposite of −6.5 and the absolute value of −6.5 the same?

   Give both. _____

2. Are the opposite of $3\dfrac{2}{5}$ and the absolute value of $3\dfrac{2}{5}$ the same?

   Give both. _____

3. Write a rational number whose opposite and absolute value are

   the same. _____

4. Write a rational number whose opposite and absolute value are

   opposites. _____

LESSON 3-3

Comparing and Ordering Rational Numbers

Practice and Problem Solving: A/B

Write each fraction as a decimal. Round to the nearest hundredth if necessary.

1. $\frac{3}{8}$ ___

2. $\frac{7}{5}$ ___

3. $\frac{21}{7}$ ___

4. $\frac{5}{3}$ ___

Write each decimal as a fraction or mixed number in simplest form.

5. 0.55 ___

6. 10.6 ___

7. –7.08 ___

Write the numbers in order from least to greatest.

8. 0.5, 0.05, $\frac{5}{8}$ _____

9. 1.3, $1\frac{1}{3}$, 1.34 _____

10. 2.07, $2\frac{7}{10}$, 2.67, –2.67 _____

Solve.

11. Out of 45 times at bat, Raul got 19 hits. Find Raul's batting average as

 a decimal rounded to the nearest thousandth. _____

12. Karen's batting average was 0.444. She was at bat 45 times. How

 many hits did she get? _____

13. To have batting averages over 0.500, how may hits in 45 times at bat

 would Raul and Karen need? _____

14. A car travels at 65 miles per hour. Going through construction, it

 travels at $\frac{3}{5}$ this speed. Write this fraction as a decimal and find the

 speed. _____

15. A city's sales tax is 0.07. Write this decimal as a fraction and tell how

 many cents of tax are on each dollar. _____

16. A ream of paper contains 500 sheets of paper. Norm has 373 sheets
 of paper left from a ream. Express the portion of a ream Norm has as a

 fraction and as a decimal. _____

LESSON 3-3

Comparing and Ordering Rational Numbers
Reteach

You can write decimals as fractions or mixed numbers. A place value table will help you read the decimal. Remember the decimal point is read as the word "and."

To write 0.47 as a fraction, first think about the decimal in words.

Ones	Tenths	Hundredths	Thousandths	Ten Thousandths
0	4	7		

0.47 is read "forty-seven hundredths." The place value of the decimal tells you the denominator is 100.

$$0.47 = \frac{47}{100}$$

To write 8.3 as a mixed number, first think about the decimal in words.

Ones	Tenths	Hundredths	Thousandths	Ten Thousandths
8	3			

8.3 is read "eight and three tenths." The place value of the decimal tells you the denominator is 10. The decimal point is read as the word "and."

$$8.3 = 8\frac{3}{10}$$

Write each decimal as a fraction or mixed number.

1. 0.61 ____   2. 3.43 ____   3. 0.009 ____   4. 4.7 ____

5. 1.5 ____   6. 0.13 ____   7. 5.002 ____   8. 0.021 ____

LESSON 4-1

Applying GCF and LCM to Fraction Operations

Practice and Problem Solving: A/B

Multiply. Use the greatest common factor to write each answer in simplest form.

1. $\frac{2}{3} \cdot \frac{6}{7}$　　　　2. $\frac{3}{4} \cdot \frac{2}{3}$　　　　3. $\frac{8}{21} \cdot \frac{7}{10}$

_____　　_____　　_____

4. $24 \cdot \frac{5}{6}$　　　　5. $32 \cdot \frac{3}{8}$　　　　6. $21 \cdot \frac{3}{7}$

_____　　_____　　_____

Add or subtract. Use the least common multiple as the denominator.

7. $\frac{4}{15} + \frac{5}{6}$　　　　8. $\frac{5}{12} - \frac{3}{20}$　　　　9. $\frac{3}{5} + \frac{3}{20}$

_____　　_____　　_____

10. $\frac{5}{8} - \frac{5}{24}$　　　　11. $3\frac{5}{12} + 1\frac{3}{8}$　　　　12. $2\frac{9}{10} - 1\frac{7}{18}$

_____　　_____　　_____

Solve.

13. Louis spent 12 hours last week practicing guitar. If $\frac{1}{4}$ of the time was spent practicing chords, how much time did Louis spend practicing chords?

_____

14. Angie and her friends ate $\frac{3}{4}$ of a pizza. Her brother Joe ate $\frac{2}{3}$ of what was left. How much of the original pizza did Joe eat?

_____

Applying GCF and LCM to Fraction Operations

LESSON 4-1

Reteach

How to Multiply a Fraction by a Fraction

$$\frac{2}{3} \cdot \frac{3}{8}$$

$$\frac{2}{3} \cdot \frac{3}{8} = \frac{6}{} \qquad \text{Multiply numerators.}$$

$$\frac{2}{3} \cdot \frac{3}{8} = \frac{6}{24} \qquad \text{Multiply denominators.}$$

$$\frac{6 \div 6}{24 \div 6} = \frac{1}{4} \qquad \text{Divide by the greatest common factor (GCF).}$$

The GCF of 6 and 24 is 6.

How to Add or Subtract Fractions

$$\frac{5}{6} + \frac{11}{15}$$

$$\frac{25}{30} + \frac{22}{30} \qquad \text{Rewrite over the least common multiple (LCM).}$$

The least common multiple of 6 and 15 is 30.

$$\frac{25}{30} + \frac{22}{30} = \frac{47}{30} \qquad \text{Add the numerators.}$$

$$= 1\frac{17}{30} \qquad \text{If the sum is an improper fraction, rewrite it as a mixed number.}$$

Multiply. Use the greatest common factor.

1. $\dfrac{3}{4} \cdot \dfrac{7}{9}$

2. $\dfrac{2}{7} \cdot \dfrac{7}{9}$

3. $\dfrac{7}{11} \cdot \dfrac{22}{28}$

_____

_____

_____

4. $8 \cdot \dfrac{3}{10}$

5. $\dfrac{4}{9} \cdot \dfrac{3}{4}$

6. $\dfrac{3}{7} \cdot \dfrac{2}{3}$

_____

_____

_____

Add or subtract. Use the least common multiple.

7. $\dfrac{7}{9} + \dfrac{5}{12}$

8. $\dfrac{21}{24} - \dfrac{3}{8}$

9. $\dfrac{11}{15} + \dfrac{7}{12}$

_____

_____

_____

LESSON 4-2	**Dividing Fractions**

Practice and Problem Solving: A/B

Find the reciprocal.

1. $\dfrac{5}{7}$ _____

2. $\dfrac{3}{4}$ _____

3. $\dfrac{3}{5}$ _____

4. $\dfrac{1}{10}$ _____

5. $\dfrac{4}{9}$ _____

6. $\dfrac{13}{14}$ _____

7. $\dfrac{7}{12}$ _____

8. $\dfrac{3}{10}$ _____

9. $\dfrac{5}{8}$ _____

Divide. Write each answer in simplest form.

10. $\dfrac{5}{6} \div \dfrac{1}{2}$ _____

11. $\dfrac{7}{8} \div \dfrac{2}{3}$ _____

12. $\dfrac{9}{10} \div \dfrac{3}{4}$ _____

13. $\dfrac{3}{4} \div 9$ _____

14. $\dfrac{6}{9} \div \dfrac{6}{7}$ _____

15. $\dfrac{5}{6} \div \dfrac{3}{10}$ _____

16. $\dfrac{5}{6} \div \dfrac{3}{4}$ _____

17. $\dfrac{5}{8} \div \dfrac{3}{5}$ _____

18. $\dfrac{21}{32} \div \dfrac{7}{8}$ _____

Solve.

19. Mrs. Marks has $\dfrac{3}{4}$ pound of cheese to use making sandwiches.

She uses about $\dfrac{1}{32}$ pound of cheese on each sandwich. How many

sandwiches can she make with the cheese she has?

_____

20. In England, mass is measured in units called *stones*. One pound

equals $\dfrac{1}{14}$ of a stone. A cat weighs $\dfrac{3}{4}$ stone. How many pounds does

the cat weigh?

_____

21. Typographers measure font sizes in units called *points*. One point is

equal to $\dfrac{1}{72}$ inch. Esmeralda is typing a research paper on her

computer. She wants the text on the title page to be $\dfrac{1}{2}$ inch tall. What

font size should she use?

_____

LESSON 4-2
Dividing Fractions
Reteach

Two numbers are reciprocals if their product is 1.

$\dfrac{2}{3}$ and $\dfrac{3}{2}$ are reciprocals because $\dfrac{2}{3} \cdot \dfrac{3}{2} = \dfrac{6}{6} = 1$.

Dividing by a number is the same as multiplying by its reciprocal.

$$\dfrac{1}{4} \div \dfrac{1}{2} = \dfrac{1}{2} \qquad \longrightarrow \qquad \dfrac{1}{4} \cdot \dfrac{2}{1} = \dfrac{1}{2}$$

So, you can use reciprocals to divide by fractions.

Find $\dfrac{2}{3} \div \dfrac{1}{4}$.

First, rewrite the expression as a multiplication expression.

Use the reciprocal of the divisor: $\dfrac{1}{4} \cdot \dfrac{4}{1} = 1$.

$$\dfrac{2}{3} \div \dfrac{1}{4} = \dfrac{2}{3} \cdot \dfrac{4}{1}$$
$$= \dfrac{8}{3}$$
$$= 2\dfrac{2}{3}$$

Think: 6 thirds is 2, and 2 of the 8 thirds are left over.

Rewrite each division expression as a multiplication expression. Then find the value of the expression. Write each answer in simplest form.

1. $\dfrac{1}{4} \div \dfrac{1}{3}$

2. $\dfrac{1}{2} \div \dfrac{1}{4}$

3. $\dfrac{3}{8} \div \dfrac{1}{2}$

4. $\dfrac{1}{3} \div \dfrac{3}{4}$

_____   _____   _____   _____

Divide. Write each answer in simplest form.

5. $\dfrac{1}{5} \div \dfrac{1}{2}$

6. $\dfrac{1}{6} \div \dfrac{2}{3}$

7. $\dfrac{1}{8} \div \dfrac{2}{5}$

8. $\dfrac{1}{8} \div \dfrac{1}{2}$

_____   _____   _____   _____

LESSON
4-3

Dividing Mixed Numbers

Practice and Problem Solving: A/B

Find the reciprocal. Show that the product of the mixed number and its reciprocal is 1.

1. $10\frac{1}{2}$

2. $6\frac{3}{7}$

3. $2\frac{8}{9}$

_____

_____

_____

4. $15\frac{1}{4}$

5. $9\frac{2}{3}$

6. $7\frac{5}{8}$

_____

_____

_____

Divide. Write each answer in simplest form.

7. $\frac{8}{10} \div 1\frac{5}{6}$

8. $2 \div 1\frac{6}{7}$

9. $3\frac{3}{5} \div 2\frac{1}{4}$

_____

_____

_____

10. $4\frac{1}{2} \div 2\frac{3}{8}$

11. $5\frac{5}{6} \div 3\frac{1}{6}$

12. $\frac{11}{12} \div 2\frac{5}{8}$

_____

_____

_____

13. $1\frac{9}{13} \div \frac{3}{8}$

14. $6\frac{4}{5} \div 3\frac{2}{9}$

15. $9\frac{2}{3} \div 6\frac{8}{9}$

_____

_____

_____

Write each situation as a division problem. Then solve.

16. A concrete patio is $5\frac{2}{3}$ feet wide. It has an area of $36\frac{5}{6}$ square feet.

    Is the concrete slab long enough to fit a 7-foot picnic table without placing the table along the diagonal of the patio? Explain.

_____

17. The area of a mirror is 225 square inches, and its width is $13\frac{3}{4}$ inches.

    Will the mirror fit in a space that is 15 inches by 16 inches? Explain.

_____

18. Barney has $16\frac{1}{5}$ yards of fabric. To make an elf costume, he needs

    $5\frac{2}{5}$ yards of fabric. How many costumes can Barney make?

_____

LESSON 4-3

Dividing Mixed Numbers

Reteach

Two numbers are **reciprocals** if their product is 1.

$\dfrac{7}{3}$ and $\dfrac{3}{7}$ are reciprocals because $\dfrac{7}{3} \times \dfrac{3}{7} = 1$.

Write a mixed number as an improper fraction to find its reciprocal.

$2\dfrac{3}{4}$ and $\dfrac{4}{11}$ are reciprocals because $2\dfrac{3}{4} = \dfrac{11}{4}$ and $\dfrac{11}{4} \times \dfrac{4}{11} = 1$.

To find $2\dfrac{3}{4} \div 1\dfrac{3}{4}$, first rewrite the mixed numbers as improper fractions.

$$\dfrac{11}{4} \div \dfrac{7}{4}$$

Next, rewrite the expression as a multiplication expression and replace the divisor with its reciprocal.

$$\dfrac{11}{4} \times \dfrac{4}{7}$$

Solve. Write your answer in simplest form.

$$2\dfrac{3}{4} \div 1\dfrac{3}{4} = \dfrac{11}{4} \div \dfrac{7}{4} = \dfrac{11}{4} \times \dfrac{4}{7} = \dfrac{11}{7} = 1\dfrac{4}{7}$$

Find the reciprocal.

1. $\dfrac{9}{14}$

2. $3\dfrac{1}{2}$

3. $10\dfrac{2}{3}$

_____   _____   _____

Complete the division. Write each answer in simplest form.

4. $3\dfrac{3}{5} \div 2\dfrac{1}{4}$

$= \dfrac{18}{5} \div \dfrac{}{4}$

$= \dfrac{}{5} \times \dfrac{}{9}$

_____

5. $1\dfrac{1}{2} \div 1\dfrac{1}{4}$

$= \dfrac{3}{2} \div \dfrac{}{4}$

$= \dfrac{}{} \times \dfrac{}{}$

_____

6. $\dfrac{5}{12} \div 1\dfrac{7}{8}$

$= \dfrac{}{12} \div \dfrac{}{8}$

$= \dfrac{}{} \times \dfrac{}{}$

_____

7. $3\dfrac{1}{8} \div \dfrac{1}{2}$

_____

8. $1\dfrac{1}{6} \div 2\dfrac{2}{3}$

_____

9. $2 \div 1\dfrac{1}{5}$

_____

LESSON 4-4

Solving Multistep Problems with Fractions and Mixed Numbers
Practice and Problem Solving: A/B

Solve. Show your work.

1. After a holiday dinner, there are $3\frac{1}{3}$ apple pies left and $2\frac{5}{6}$ pumpkin pies left.

   a. How much more apple pie than pumpkin pie is left?

   _____

   b. Tom ate $\frac{1}{2}$ of the leftovers. How much pie in all did he eat?

   _____

2. An angelfish was $1\frac{1}{2}$ inches long when it was bought. Now it is $2\frac{1}{3}$ inches long.

   a. How much has the angelfish grown? _____

   b. An inch is $\frac{1}{12}$ of a foot. How much has the angelfish grown in feet? _____

3. There was a 6 square-foot piece of wrapping paper for a birthday present. It takes $3\frac{3}{8}$ square feet of the paper to wrap the present. How many pieces of 6 square-foot paper are needed to wrap 3 of these presents?

   _____

4. Today, a bicycle rider rode her bike $5\frac{1}{2}$ miles. Yesterday, she rode $6\frac{1}{4}$ miles. The difference in length between the two rides is what fraction of the longer ride?

   _____

5. A survey by the state health department found that the average person ate 208 pounds of vegetables last year and $125\frac{5}{8}$ pounds of fruit. What fraction of the total pounds of fruit and vegetables do the pounds of fruits represent?

   _____

Solving Multistep Problems with Fractions and Mixed Numbers
Reteach

In order to solve some problems involving mixed numbers, you will have to rewrite the mixed number as a whole number and an improper fraction. For example, $2\frac{1}{3}$ can be rewritten as $1\frac{4}{3}$. The two numbers are the same because $2\frac{1}{3} = 1 + 1\frac{1}{3} = \frac{3}{3} + 1\frac{1}{3} = 1 + \frac{3}{3} + \frac{1}{3}$. This step is necessary when subtracting mixed numbers as shown here.

Example

After an office party, $4\frac{1}{3}$ pizzas are left. A day later, there are $1\frac{5}{6}$ pizzas left. How much pizza was eaten during the day after the party? One third of the pizza eaten on the day after the party was pepperoni. How much of the day-old pizza eaten was pepperoni?

Solution:

First, change the denominator to the common denominator of 6:

$4\frac{1}{3} = 4\frac{2}{6}$

Then, write the subtraction problem: $4\frac{2}{6} - 1\frac{5}{6}$

Since the fraction with 4 is less than the fraction with 1, write $4\frac{2}{6}$ as $1 + 3\frac{2}{6}$ and write 1 as $\frac{6}{6}$ so that the subtraction problem becomes $3\frac{8}{6} - 1\frac{5}{6}$.

Subtract the whole numbers and subtract the numerators of the fractions:

$3\frac{8}{6} - 1\frac{5}{6} = 2 + \frac{3}{6}$ or $2\frac{1}{2}$; $2\frac{1}{2}$ pizzas were eaten during the next day. Of these, $\frac{1}{3}$ were pepperoni. So: $2\frac{1}{2} \cdot \frac{1}{3} = \frac{5}{2} \cdot \frac{1}{3} = \frac{5}{6}$.

On the second day, $\frac{5}{6}$ of a pepperoni pizza was eaten.

Solve by rewriting the mixed number that is being subtracted.

1. A deli ordered $6\frac{1}{2}$ wheels of cheese. Over the weekend, $3\frac{5}{8}$ wheels of cheese were sold. On Tuesday another $1\frac{3}{4}$ wheels were sold. How much cheese was left for Wednesday?

_____

LESSON 5-1

Dividing Whole Numbers

Practice and Problem Solving: A/B

Estimate each quotient by rounding the dividend and the divisor to the largest place value.

1. $585 \div 13$

2. $2,756 \div 53$

3. $22,528 \div 98$

_____   _____   _____

4. $7,790 \div 210$

5. $17,658 \div 360$

6. $916 \div 320$

_____   _____   _____

Find each quotient using long division. Show your work.

7.
$$29\overline{)1,334}$$

8.
$$92\overline{)20,884}$$

9.
$$25\overline{)18,175}$$

_____   _____   _____

Find each quotient and remainder using long division. Show your work.

10.
$$18\overline{)2,902}$$

11.
$$64\overline{)34,680}$$

12.
$$215\overline{)52,245}$$

_____   _____   _____

Solve.

13. At the museum, there were 4,050 students in attendance from a total of 15 different school districts. What was the average attendance from each school district?

_____

14. The Appalachian Trail is about 2,175 miles long. If a hiker averages 12 miles each day, how long will it take her to hike the length of the trail?

_____

LESSON 5-1

Dividing Whole Numbers

Reteach

Division is used to separate a quantity into a given number of equal parts.

It is also used to separate a quantity into parts of a specific size.

A **division algorithm** breaks division with greater numbers into a series of lesser divisions. Follow the steps for each lesser division:

Step 1: Divide and write the number in the first correct place in the quotient.

Step 2: Multiply the divisor by the number in the quotient.

Step 3: Subtract.

Step 4: Bring down the next digit in the dividend.

Repeat these steps until there are no digits from the dividend left to bring down.

Jon bought a package of 792 labels. There are 24 sheets of labels in the package.

How many labels are on each sheet?

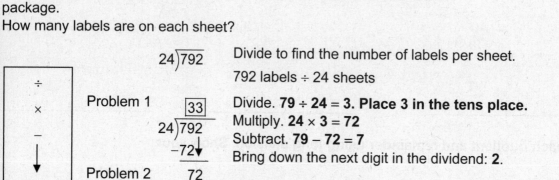

Divide to find the number of labels per sheet.

792 labels ÷ 24 sheets

Problem 1

Divide. **79 ÷ 24 = 3. Place 3 in the tens place.**

Multiply. **24 × 3 = 72**

Subtract. **79 − 72 = 7**

Bring down the next digit in the dividend: **2.**

Problem 2

Repeat the process.

Divide. **72 ÷ 24 = 3.** Place 3 in the _____ones_____ place.

Multiply. **24 × 3 = 72**

Subtract. **72 − 72 = 0**

792 ÷ 24 = 33. There are 33 labels on each sheet.

Use the 4-step process to do the division.

1. The art teacher has a box of 473 markers. She wants to distribute them evenly among 11 tables. How many markers will she put on each table?

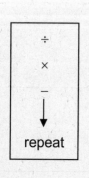

$$11\overline{)473}$$
$$\underline{-44}$$
$$33$$
$$\underline{-33}$$
$$0$$

Divide: 47 ÷ _____ = _____

Multiply: 11 × _____ = _____

Subtract: 47 − _____ = _____

Bring down the _____.

Repeat the steps.

Divide: _____ ÷ _____ = _____

Multiply: _____ × _____ = _____

Subtract: _____ − _____ = _____

Answer: _____ markers

LESSON 5-2
Adding and Subtracting Decimals
Practice and Problem Solving: A/B

Find each sum or difference.

1. $1.5 + 2.3$

_____

2. $8.9 - 5.1$

_____

3. $2.5 + 1.3 + 4.1$

_____

4. $7.25 + 8.75$

_____

5. $8.16 - 7.72$

_____

6. $3.3 + 4.5 + 2.6$

_____

7. $8.9 + 3.05$

_____

8. $10.64 - 8.8$

_____

9. $4.1 + 0.35 + 6.564$

_____

Solve.

10. Marcus is 1.5 meters tall. His sister is 0.1 meter taller than Marcus. Their father is 0.2 meter taller than his sister. How tall is their father?

_____

11. Jennifer brought $24.75 to the baseball game. She spent $12.45 on drinks and snacks. How much money does she have left over?

_____

Find the missing digit.

12.
$$\begin{array}{r} 7.089 \\ + \ 2.\square13 \\ \hline 9.502 \end{array}$$

_____

13.
$$\begin{array}{r} 16.594 \\ - \ \square.175 \\ \hline 11.419 \end{array}$$

_____

14.
$$\begin{array}{r} 6.2\square67 \\ + \ 9.75 \\ \hline 15.9867 \end{array}$$

_____

Solve.

15. A gourmet pizza café sells three sizes of pizzas. If you buy all three sizes, it costs $46.24. A medium pizza costs $15.75 and a large pizza costs $17.50. How much does the small pizza cost?

_____

16. A carpenter has three sheets of plywood that are each 6.85 feet long. A 3.4-foot piece is cut from one sheet and 0.5-foot piece is cut from another sheet. How many feet of plywood is left in all?

_____

LESSON 5-2

Adding and Subtracting Decimals
Reteach

You can use a place-value chart to help you add and subtract decimals.

Add 1.4 and 0.9.

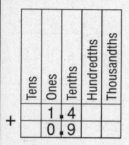

So, 1.4 + 0.9 = 2.3.

Subtract 2.4 from 3.1.

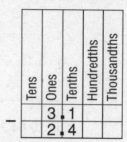

So, 3.1 − 2.4 = 0.7.

Find each sum or difference.

1.

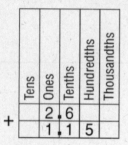

_____

2.

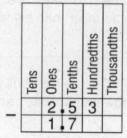

_____

3. 4.3 + 1.4

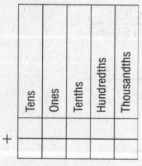

_____

4. 14.4 − 3.8

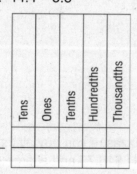

_____

5. 7.3 + 8.5

_____

6. 12.34 − 6.9

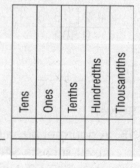

_____

Estimate the answers to Exercises 3–6 by rounding to the nearest whole number. Compare your estimate to the exact answers.

7. 4.3 + 1.4

_____

8. 14.4 − 3.8

_____

9. 7.3 + 8.5

_____

10. 12.34 − 6.9

_____

LESSON
5-3

Multiplying Decimals

Practice and Problem Solving: A/B

Show the decimal multiplication on the grids. Find the product.

1. 0.2×0.6 _____

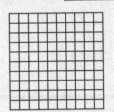

2. 0.3×0.7 _____

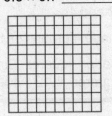

Draw an area model to represent the multiplication problems below. Find the product.

3. $1.2 \times 3.3 =$ _____

4. $4.1 \times 2.1 =$ _____

Multiply.

5.   0.1
   $\times\, 0.2$

6.   0.9
   $\times\, 6$

7.   0.3
   $\times\, 0.8$

8.   1.6
   $\times\, 2.9$

9. $1.5 \times 0.41 =$

10. $0.24 \times 2.68 =$

11. $3.13 \times 4.69 =$

12. $5.48 \times 15.12 =$

_____

_____

_____

_____

Solve.

13. Each basket can hold 2.5 pounds of apples. How many pounds can 7 baskets hold?

_____

14. Canvas cloth costs $7.50 per square meter. How much will 3.5 square meters of canvas cost?

_____

LESSON 5-3 Multiplying Decimals
Reteach

You can use a model to help you multiply a decimal by a whole number.

Find the product of 0.12 and 4.

Use a 10-by-10 grid. Shade 4 groups of 12 squares.

Count the number of shaded squares. Since you have shaded 48 of the 100 squares, $0.12 \times 4 = 0.48$.

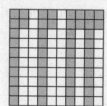

Find each product.

1. 0.23×3 2. 0.41×2 3. 0.01×5 4. 0.32×2

_____   _____   _____   _____

5. 0.15×3 6. 0.42×2 7. 0.04×8 8. 0.22×4

_____   _____   _____   _____

You can also use a model to help you multiply a decimal by a decimal.

Find the product of 0.8 and 0.4.

Step 1   Shade 8 tenths of the figure.

Step 2   Shade darker 4 tenths of the shaded area.

Step 3   How many squares have you shaded twice?

You have twice shaded 32 of the squares.

So, $0.8 \times 0.4 = 0.32$.

Find each product.

9. 0.2×0.8 10. 0.7×0.9 11. 0.5×0.5 12. 0.3×0.6

_____   _____   _____   _____

13. 0.5×0.2 14. 0.4×0.4 15. 0.1×0.9 16. 0.4×0.7

_____   _____   _____   _____

LESSON 5-4

Dividing Decimals
Practice and Problem Solving: A/B

Use decimal grids to find each quotient. First, shade the grid. Then, separate the model to show the correct number of equal parts.

1. $3.6 \div 1.2$

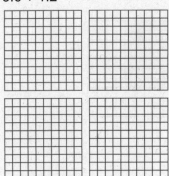

_____

2. $3.27 \div 3$

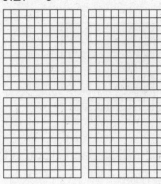

_____

Find each quotient.

3. $9.5\overline{)142.5}$

_____

4. $3\overline{)39.6}$

_____

5. $2\overline{)10.88}$

_____

6. $10.5 \div 1.5$

_____

7. $9.75 \div 1.3$

_____

8. $37.5 \div 2.5$

_____

Estimate each quotient to the nearest whole number. Then, find the actual quotient.

9. $0.9\overline{)3.78}$

_____

10. $2.5\overline{)36}$

_____

11. $0.25\overline{)7}$

_____

12. $9.5\overline{)142.5}$

_____

Solve.

13. A camera attached to a telescope photographs a star's image once every 0.045 seconds. How many complete images can the camera capture in 3 seconds?

_____

14. A geologist noticed that land along a fault line moved 24.8 centimeters over the past 175 years. On average, how much did the land move each year?

_____

LESSON 5-4

Dividing Decimals

Reteach

You can use decimal grids to help you divide by whole numbers.

To divide 0.35 by 7, first shade in a decimal grid to show thirty-five hundredths.

0.35 ÷ 7 means "divide 0.35 into 7 equal groups." Show this on the decimal grid.

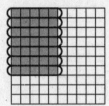

The number of units in each group is the quotient.

So, 0.35 ÷ 7 = 0.05.

Find each quotient.

1. 0.6 ÷ 5

2. 0.78 ÷ 6

3. 0.32 ÷ 4

4. 0.99 ÷ 0.0033

_____ _____ _____ _____

You can use powers of 10 to help you divide a decimal by a decimal.

Divide 0.048 by 0.12.

Notice that 0.12 has two decimal places.
To make this a whole number, multiply by 100.

0.048 ÷ 0.12 ⟶ 0.12 • 100 = 12   0.048 • 100 = 4.8

Then divide.

4.8 ÷ 12

$$\frac{0.4}{12)\overline{4.8}}$$
$$\underline{4\ 8}$$
$$0$$

Step 1: Divide as you would with a whole number.

Step 2: Think 48 ÷ 12 = 4.

Step 3: Place the decimal point in the quotient.
Add a zero as necessary.

So, 0.048 ÷ 0.12 = 0.4.

Find each quotient.

5. 0.4)‾0.08

6. 0.9)‾0.63

7. 0.008)‾0.4

8. 0.04)‾0.032

_____ _____ _____ _____

LESSON
5-5

Applying Operations with Rational Numbers
Practice and Problem Solving: A/B

Solve.

1. Four friends equally shared the cost of supplies for a picnic. The supplies cost $12.40. How much did each pay?

   _____

2. Twenty people are going by van to a movie. Each van seats 8 people. How many vans are needed to take everyone?

   _____

3. Plastic forks come in packs of 6. You need 40 forks for a party. How many packs of forks should you buy?

   _____

4. Kesha spent a total of $9.60 on new shoelaces. Each pair cost $1.20. How many pairs of shoelaces did she buy?

   _____

5. Horses are measured in units called hands. One inch equals $\frac{1}{4}$ hand. The average Clydesdale is $17\frac{1}{5}$ hands tall. What is this height in inches? In feet?

   _____

6. A banana bread recipe calls for $\frac{3}{4}$ cup butter. One tablespoon equals $\frac{1}{16}$ cup. How many tablespoons of butter are needed to make the banana bread?

   _____

7. Cindy works part-time and earns $5.75 an hour. One year she worked 50 weeks and averaged 12.4 hours of work per week. About how much money did she earn that year?

   _____

8. At a gymnastics competition, Joey scored 9.4, 9.7, 9.9, and 9.8. Carlos scored 9.5, 9.2, 9.7, and 9.6. Who had the greater average score? By how many points was his score greater?

   _____

9. A granola recipe calls for $2\frac{1}{3}$ cups of almonds. A bag of almonds contains 2 cups. To make $2\frac{1}{2}$ batches of granola, Ali buys 5 bags of almonds. How many cups of almonds will he have left over?

   _____

10. At a zoo, 3 pandas eat a total of $181\frac{1}{2}$ pounds of bamboo shoots each day. The male panda eats 3 times as much as the baby. The female eats twice as much as the baby. How many pounds of bamboo shoots does the female panda eat?

   _____

LESSON 5-5

Applying Operations with Rational Numbers
Reteach

When a word problem involves fractions or decimals, use these four steps to help you decide which operation to use.

Tanya has $13\frac{1}{2}$ feet of ribbon. To giftwrap boxes, she needs to cut it into $\frac{7}{8}$-foot lengths. How many lengths can Tanya cut?

Step 1	Read the problem carefully. What is asked for?	The number of lengths is asked for.
Step 2	Think of a simpler problem that includes only whole numbers.	Tanya has 12 feet of ribbon. She wants to cut it into 2-foot lengths. How many lengths can she cut?
Step 3	How would you solve the simpler problem?	Divide 12 by 2. Tanya can cut 6 lengths.
Step 4	Use the same reasoning with the original problem.	Divide $13\frac{1}{2}$ by $\frac{7}{8}$. Tanya can cut 15 lengths.

Tell whether you should multiply or divide. Then solve the problem.

1. Jan has $37.50. Tickets to a concert cost $5.25 each. How many tickets can Jan buy?

_____

2. Jon has $45.00. He plans to spend $\frac{4}{5}$ of his money on sports equipment. How much will he spend?

_____

3. Ricki has 76.8 feet of cable. She plans to cut it into 7 pieces. How long will each piece be?

_____

4. Roger has $2\frac{1}{2}$ cups of butter. A recipe for a loaf of bread requires $\frac{3}{4}$ cup of butter. How many loaves can Roger bake?

_____

LESSON 6-1 Ratios

Practice and Problem Solving: A/B

The number of animals at the zoo is shown in the table. Write each ratio in three different ways.

Animals in the Zoo	
Elephants	12
Giraffes	8
Lions	9
Seals	10
Otters	16

1. lions to elephants

   _____

2. giraffes to otters

   _____

3. lions to seals

   _____

4. seals to elephants

   _____

5. elephants to lions

   _____

Write three equivalent ratios for the given ratio.

6. $\frac{4}{3}$ _____

7. $\frac{12}{14}$ _____

8. $\frac{6}{9}$ _____

Find three ratios equivalent to the ratio described in each situation.

9. The ratio of cats to dogs in a park is 3 to 4. _____

10. The ratio of rainy days to sunny days is $\frac{5}{7}$. _____

11. The ratio of protein to fiber in a granola bar is $\frac{9}{2}$. _____

12. The ratio of clown fish to angelfish at a pet store is 5:4. The ratio of angelfish to goldfish is 4:3. There are 60 clown fish at the pet store.

    a. How many angelfish are there? _____

    b. How many goldfish are there? _____

Ratios
Reteach

A ratio is a comparison of two quantities by division.

To compare the number of times vowels are used to the number of time consonants are used in the word "mathematics," first find each quantity.

Number of times vowels are used: 4

Number of times consonants are used: 7

Then write the comparison as a ratio, using the quantities in the same order as they appear in the word expression. There are three ways to write a ratio.

$\frac{4}{7}$ 4 to 7   4:7

Write each ratio.

1. days in May to days in a year

_____

2. sides of a triangle to sides of a square

_____

Equivalent ratios are ratios that name the same comparison.

The ratio of inches in a foot to inches in a yard is $\frac{12}{36}$. To find equivalent ratios, divide or multiply the numerator and denominator by the same number.

$$\frac{12}{36} = \frac{12 \div 3}{36 \div 3} = \frac{4}{12} \qquad \frac{12}{36} = \frac{12 \cdot 2}{36 \cdot 2} = \frac{24}{72}$$

So, $\frac{12}{36}$, $\frac{4}{12}$, and $\frac{24}{72}$ are equivalent ratios.

Write three equivalent ratios to compare each of the following.

3. 8 triangles to 12 circles

_____

4. 20 pencils to 25 erasers

_____

5. 5 girls to 6 boys

_____

6. 10 pants to 14 shirts

_____

Name _____ Date _____ Class _____

Rates

Practice and Problem Solving: A/B

Find the unit rate.

1. David drove 135 miles in 3 hours. _____

2. Three medium apples have about 285 calories. _____

3. A 13-ounce package of pistachios costs $5.99. _____

Use the information in the table to solve Exercises 4–6.

Morgan's favorite spaghetti sauce is available in two sizes: pint and quart. Each size and its price are shown in the table.

Size	Quantity (oz)	Price ($)
pint	16	3.98
quart	32	5.98

4. What is the unit rate to the nearest cent per ounce for each size?

   a. pint: _____   b. quart: _____

5. Which size is the better buy? _____

6. A coupon offers $1.00 off the 16-ounce size. Which size is the better buy then?

   _____

Find the unit rate to the nearest cent per ounce. Compare.

7. a. A 24-ounce box of cornflakes costs $4.59. _____

   b. A 36-ounce box of cornflakes costs $5.79. _____

   c. Which is the better buy? _____

Solve.

8. Karyn proofreads 15 pages in 2 hours for $40.

   a. What is her proofreading rate in pages per hour?

   _____

   b. How much does she receive on average for a page?

   _____

Rates

Reteach

LESSON 6-2

You can divide to find a unit rate or to determine a best buy.

A. Find the unit rate.
Karin bikes 35 miles in 7 hours.
$35 \div 7 = 5$ mph

B. Find the best buy.

2 lb
$5

4 lb
$8

10 lb
$15

BEST BUY!

$5 \div 2 = \$2.50$
per lb

$8 \div 4 = \$2.00$
per lb

$15 \div 10 = \$1.50$
per lb

Divide to find each unit rate. Show your work.

1. Jack shells 315 peanuts in 15 minutes. _____

2. Sharmila received 81 texts in 9 minutes. _____

3. Karim read 56 pages in 2 hours. _____

Find the best buy. Show your work.

4.

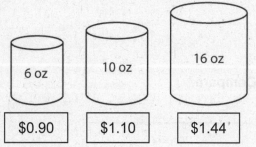

6 oz

10 oz

16 oz

$0.90

$1.10

$1.44

_____

_____

5.

Bread	Weight (oz)	Cost ($)
Whole wheat	16	2.24
Pita	20	3.60
7-grain	16	2.56

_____

_____

_____

_____

LESSON 6-3

Using Ratios and Rates to Solve Problems
Practice and Problem Solving: A/B

Solve using ratios.

1. Mark is using the ratio of 3 tablespoons of sugar to 2 tablespoons of milk in a recipe. Complete the table to show equivalent ratios if Mark decides to increase the recipe.

sugar	3	6		18	
milk	2		8		20

2. Mark's ratio is 3 tablespoons sugar to 2 tablespoons milk. Sharri is using 4 tablespoons of sugar to 3 tablespoons of milk. Eve is using 9 tablespoons of sugar to 6 tablespoons of milk. Which girl's ratio is

   equivalent to Mark's? _____

3. A school cafeteria makes cheese sauce for macaroni using 15 cups of Swiss cheese and 17 cups of cheddar cheese. Perry tries to make the sauce for a family party using 5 cups of Swiss and 7 cups of cheddar.

   Is Perry using the correct ratio? Explain. _____

   _____

4. The chess club members bought 6 tickets to a tournament for $15. How much would they have paid if all 9 members wanted to go?

   _____

5. The Khan's car averages 22 miles per gallon of gas. Predict how far

   they can travel on 5 gallons of gas. _____

6. Cafe A offers 2 free bottled waters or juices for every 20 purchased. Cafe B offers 3 free bottled waters or juices for every 25 purchased.

   a. What is Cafe A's ratio of free drinks to purchased drinks?

      _____

   b. What is Cafe B's ratio of free drinks to purchased drinks?

      _____

   c. If you purchased 50 drinks at each café, how many free drinks would you get?

      _____

LESSON 6-3

Using Ratios and Rates to Solve Problems
Reteach

You can write a ratio and make a list of equivalent ratios to compare ratios.

Find out who uses more detergent.

Terri's recipe for soap bubble liquid uses 1 cup of dishwashing detergent to 4 cups of water.

Torri's recipe for soap bubble liquid uses 1 cup of dishwashing detergent to 12 cups of water (plus some glycerin drops).

Terri's ratio of detergent to water: 1 to 4 or $\dfrac{1}{4}$

Torri's ratio of detergent to water: 1 to 12 or $\dfrac{1}{12}$

List of fractions equivalent to $\dfrac{1}{4}$: $\dfrac{1}{4}, \dfrac{2}{8}, \boxed{\dfrac{3}{12}}, \dfrac{4}{16}, \dfrac{5}{20} \cdots$

List of fractions equivalent to $\dfrac{1}{12}$: $\boxed{\dfrac{1}{12}}, \dfrac{2}{24}, \dfrac{3}{36}, \dfrac{4}{48}, \dfrac{5}{60} \cdots$

You can compare $\dfrac{3}{12}$ to $\dfrac{1}{12}, \dfrac{3}{12} > \dfrac{1}{12}$.

Terri uses much more detergent.

Use the list to compare the ratios. Circle ratios with the same denominator and compare.

1. $\dfrac{2}{3}$ and $\dfrac{3}{4}$

_____

_____

2. $\dfrac{4}{5}$ and $\dfrac{3}{7}$

_____

_____

3. Jack's recipe for oatmeal uses 3 cups of oats to 5 cups of water. Evan's recipe uses 4 cups of oats to 6 cups of water. Compare the ratios of oats to water to see who makes the thicker oatmeal. (Thicker oatmeal has a greater ratio of oats to water.) Show your work.

_____

_____

Ratios, Rates, Tables, and Graphs

LESSON 7-1

Practice and Problem Solving: A/B

Use the table to complete Exercises 1–7.

The table shows information about the packets of flavoring added to an amount of water to make soup.

Packets of Flavoring	2	5		10	
Ounces of Water	24		84		144

1. Find the rate of ounces of water needed for each packet of flavoring. Show your work.

    $\dfrac{\text{ounces of water}}{\text{packets of flavoring}} =$ _____

2. Use the unit rate to help you complete the table.

3. Graph the information in the table.

4. How much water should be added to 23 packets of flavoring?

    _____

5. Does the point (9.5, 114) make sense in this context? Explain.

    _____

    _____

    _____

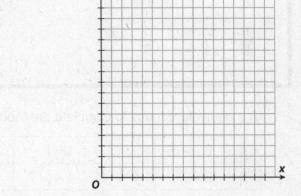

6. What are the equivalent ratios shown in the table? Complete the statement.

    $\dfrac{24}{2} = \dfrac{}{3} = \dfrac{}{5.5} = \dfrac{108}{} = \dfrac{}{15}$

7. Does the relationship shown use addition or multiplication? Explain.

    _____

    _____

LESSON 7-1

Ratios, Rates, Tables, and Graphs

Reteach

A **ratio** shows a relationship between two quantities.

Ratios are **equivalent** if they can be written as the same fraction in lowest terms.

A **rate** is a ratio that shows the relationship between two different units of measure in lowest terms.

You can make a table of equivalent ratios. You can graph the equivalent ratios.

A	4	6	10	12
B	2	3	5	6

$$\frac{4}{2} = \frac{2}{1} \qquad \frac{6}{3} = \frac{2}{1}$$

$$\frac{10}{5} = \frac{2}{1} \qquad \frac{12}{6} = \frac{2}{1}$$

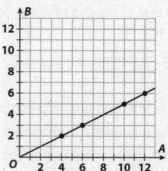

1. Use equivalent ratios to complete the table.

A	6	9			18		
B	2		4	5		7	8

2. Show the ratios are equivalent by simplifying any 4 of them.

_____

3. Find the rate of $\frac{A}{B}$ and complete the equivalent ratio: $\dfrac{69}{\rule{1cm}{0.4pt}}$.

_____

4. Use the rate to find how many As are needed for 63 Bs, then write the ratio.

_____

LESSON 7-2

Applying Ratio and Rate Reasoning

Practice and Problem Solving: A/B

Find the unknown value in each proportion. Round to the nearest tenth if needed.

1. $\dfrac{4}{5} = \dfrac{}{20}$

2. $\dfrac{3}{7} = \dfrac{}{35}$

3. $\dfrac{4}{3} = \dfrac{12}{}$

4. $\dfrac{13}{15} = \dfrac{52}{}$

Solve using equivalent ratios.

5. Wayne has a recipe on a 3-inch-by-5-inch index card that he wants to enlarge to 15 inches long. How wide will the enlargement be?

_____

6. Sharon is decreasing the size of a diagram of a leaf that is 30 centimeters long by 10 centimeters wide. If the reduced diagram is 4 centimeters wide, how long will it be?

_____

Solve using unit rates. Round to the nearest hundredth if needed.

7. A wood stove burns 4 same-sized logs in 2 hours. How many logs

does the stove burn in 8 hours? _____

8. In 2012, five U.S. postal stamps cost $2.20. How much did seven

stamps cost? _____

9. a. What is the actual distance between Saugerties and

Kingston? _____

b. Catskill is 15 miles from Saugerties. What would the

distance on the map be? _____

c. On another map, the distance between Saugerties and Kingston is 2 inches. What would the distance from

Saugerties to Catskill be on this map? _____

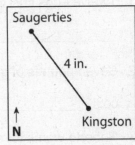

Scale: 1 in. = 2.5 mi.

10. The scale of a map is 1 in. : 250 miles. City A is 378 miles from City B. To the nearest tenth, how far is its distance on the map?

_____

LESSON 7-2

Applying Ratio and Rate Reasoning
Reteach

You can solve problems with proportions in two ways.

A. Use equivalent ratios.

Hanna can wrap 3 boxes in 15 minutes.
How many boxes can she wrap in 45 minutes?

$$\frac{3}{15} = \frac{}{45}$$

$3 \times 3 = ?$
$15 \times 3 = 45$

$$\frac{3 \cdot 3}{15 \cdot 3} = \frac{9}{45}$$

Hanna can wrap 9 boxes in 45 minutes.

B. Use unit rates.

Dan can cycle 7 miles in 28 minutes.
How long will it take him to cycle 9 miles?

$$\frac{28 \text{ min}}{7 \text{ mi}} = \frac{}{1 \text{ mi}}$$

Divide by 7.

$$\frac{28}{7} = \frac{28 \div 7}{1} = \frac{4}{1}, \text{ or 4 minutes per mile}$$

To cycle 9 miles, it will take Dan 9×4, or 36 minutes.

Solve each proportion. Use equivalent ratios or unit rates. Round to the nearest hundredth if needed.

1. Twelve eggs cost $2.04. How much would 18 eggs cost?

   _____

2. Seven pounds of grapes cost $10.43. How much would 3 pounds

   cost? _____

3. Roberto wants to reduce a drawing that is 12 inches long by 9 inches wide. If his new drawing is 8 inches long, how wide will it be?

   _____

LESSON 7-3 Converting within Measurement Systems

Practice and Problem Solving: A/B

Use proportions to convert.

1. 4 feet to inches

_____

2. 6 quarts to gallons

_____

3. 5 kilometers to meters

_____

4. 2,000 grams to kilograms

_____

Use conversion factors to convert. Write the factor you used.

5. 5 quarts to cups

_____

6. 600 centimeters to meters

_____

Solve.

7. Denver is called the Mile-High City because it is at an altitude of 1 mile.

   How many feet is this? _____

8. The distance from the library to the park is 0.7 kilometers.

   How many meters is this? _____

9. Marcus has three dowels with the lengths shown in the table.
   Complete the table to give each length in inches, feet, and yards.

Dowel	in.	ft	yd
A	36		
B		$5\frac{1}{2}$	
C			$2\frac{1}{2}$

10. Cameron wants to measure a poster frame, but he only has a sheet of

    paper that is $8\frac{1}{2}$ by 11 inches.

    a. He lays the long edge of the paper along the long edge of the frame several times
       and finds the frame is 4 papers long. How long is this in inches?

       _____ In feet? _____

    b. He lays the short edge of the paper along the short edge of the frame several times
       and finds the frame is 3 papers wide. How long is this in inches?

       _____ In feet? _____

11. How would you convert 3 yards 2 feet to inches?

_____

LESSON
7-3
Converting within Measurement Systems
Reteach

You can use a bar model to convert measurements.

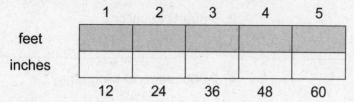

$\dfrac{1}{12} = \dfrac{3}{36}$ so 3 feet = 36 inches

$\dfrac{1,000}{1} = \dfrac{4,000}{4}$ so 4,000 g = 4 kg

1. Draw a bar model for converting feet to yards.

2. Draw a bar model for converting cups to fluid ounces.

3. Do you think a bar model would be a good model for converting miles to feet? Explain.

_____

_____

_____

LESSON 7-4

Converting Between Measurement Systems

Practice and Problem Solving: A/B

Length	Mass	Capacity
1 inch = 2.54 centimeters 1 foot ≈ 0.305 meter 1 yard ≈ 0.914 meter 1 mile ≈ 1.61 kilometers	1 ounce ≈ 28.4 grams 1 pound ≈ 0.454 kilogram	1 fluid ounce ≈ 29.6 milliliters 1 quart ≈ 0.946 liter 1 gallon ≈ 3.79 liters

Use a conversion factor to convert each measurement. Round your answer to the nearest hundredth.

1. A driveway is 40 yards long. About how many meters long is it?

   _____

2. An ice cube is made of 5 fluid ounces of water. About how many

   milliliters of water does it take to make the ice cube? _____

3. Steven bagged 52 pounds of potatoes. About what is that measure in

   kilograms? _____

4. It is 7 kilometers from Kerry's house to the mall. About what is that

   distance in miles? _____

5. A cooler holds 15 liters of water. About how many gallons does it hold?

   _____

6. Mia's cat weighs 13 pounds, 7 ounces. About what is that weight in

   kilograms? (Hint: 1 kilogram = 1,000 grams) _____

7. D'Quan's grandmother made a quilt for his bed. The quilt is
   2.44 meters long and 1.83 meters wide. What is the area of the quilt in

   square feet? _____

8. It is recommended that an adult drink 64 fluid ounces of water every
   day. Josey has already consumed 700 milliliters of water. How many

   more liters should he drink today? _____

LESSON 7-4

Converting Between Measurement Systems
Reteach

Sometimes you have to convert measurements from one system of measurement to another. You can use this conversion chart to help you change from customary units to metric units.

Length	Mass	Capacity
1 inch = 2.54 centimeters 1 foot ≈ 0.305 meter 1 yard ≈ 0.914 meter 1 mile ≈ 1.61 kilometers	1 ounce ≈ 28.4 grams 1 pound ≈ 0.454 kilogram	1 fluid ounce ≈ 29.6 milliliters 1 quart ≈ 0.946 liter 1 gallon ≈ 3.79 liters

To change from inches to centimeters, multiply the number of inches by the factor in the chart: 1 inch = 2.54 centimeters.

$$8 \text{ inches} \times 2.54 = 20.32 \text{ centimeters}$$

Most conversions are approximate. This is shown by the symbol ≈.

Find each conversion factor in the chart.

1. To convert from feet to meters, multiply by _____

2. To convert from quarts to liters, multiply by _____

3. To convert from pounds to kilograms, multiply by _____

4. To convert from gallons to liters, multiply by _____

Use a conversion factor from the chart to change each measurement.

5. 9 yards ≈ _____ meters

6. 4 ounces ≈ _____ grams

7. 12 fluid ounces ≈ _____ milliliters

8. 3 miles ≈ _____ kilometers

9. 24 pounds ≈ _____ kilograms

10. 7 gallons ≈ _____ liters

LESSON 8-1

Understanding Percent

Practice and Problem Solving: A/B

Write each percent as a fraction in simplest form and as a decimal to the nearest hundredth.

1. 30% _____

2. 42% _____

3. 18% _____

_____

_____

_____

4. 35% _____

5. 100% _____

6. 29% _____

_____

_____

_____

7. 56% _____

8. $66\frac{2}{3}$% _____

9. 25% _____

_____

_____

_____

Write each decimal or fraction as a percent.

10. 0.03 _____

11. 0.92 _____

12. 0.18 _____

13. $\frac{2}{5}$ _____

14. $\frac{23}{25}$ _____

15. $\frac{7}{10}$ _____

Solve.

16. Bradley completed $\frac{3}{5}$ of his homework. What percent of his homework

   does he still need to complete? _____

17. After reading a book for English class, 100 students were asked whether or not they enjoyed it. Nine twenty-fifths of the class did not like the book. How many students liked the book?

   _____

18. At a concert, 20% of the people are wearing black dresses or suits, $\frac{1}{4}$ are wearing navy, 0.35 are wearing brown, and the rest are wearing a variety of colors (other). Write the percent, fraction, and decimal for each color clothing.

   black _____

   navy _____

   brown _____

   other _____

LESSON
8-1

Understanding Percent
Reteach

A. A percent is a ratio of a number to 100. Percent means "per hundred."
To write 38% as a fraction, write a fraction with a denominator of 100.

$$\frac{38}{100}$$

Then write the fraction in simplest form.

$$\frac{38}{100} = \frac{38 \div 2}{100 \div 2} = \frac{19}{50}$$

So, $38\% = \frac{19}{50}$.

B. To write 38% as a decimal, first write it as fraction.

$$38\% = \frac{38}{100}$$

$\frac{38}{100}$ means "38 divided by 100."

```
        0.38
  100 )38.00
       −300
        800
       −800
          0
```

So, $38\% = 0.38$.

Write each percent as a fraction in simplest form.

1. 43%   2. 72%   3. 88%   4. 35%

_____   _____   _____   _____

Write each percent as a decimal.

5. 64%   6. 92%   7. 73%   8. 33%

_____   _____   _____   _____

Percents, Fractions, and Decimals
Practice and Problem Solving: A/B

Write each decimal as a percent.

1. 0.17

2. 0.56

3. 0.04

4. 0.7

_____

_____

_____

_____

5. 0.025

6. 0.803

7. 1.3

8. 2.10

_____

_____

_____

_____

Write each fraction as a percent.

9. $\frac{13}{50}$

10. $\frac{3}{5}$

11. $\frac{3}{20}$

12. $\frac{127}{100}$

_____

_____

_____

_____

13. $\frac{5}{8}$

14. $\frac{45}{90}$

15. $\frac{7}{5}$

16. $\frac{19}{25}$

_____

_____

_____

_____

Order the numbers from least to greatest.

17. 0.3, $\frac{19}{50}$, 22%

18. 11%, $\frac{1}{8}$, $\frac{2}{25}$

19. $\frac{5}{8}$, 0.675, 5%

_____

_____

_____

20. 1.25, 0.51, 250%

21. $\frac{350}{100}$, 0.351, 27%

22. $\frac{4}{8}$, 0.05, 51%

_____

_____

_____

23. The police use a speed gun to monitor one part of a highway. During one hour, 6 out of 25 cars were traveling above the speed limit. What percent of the cars were traveling above the speed limit?

_____

24. At Oaknoll School, 90 out of 270 students own computers. What percent of students at Oaknoll School do not own computers? Round to the nearest tenth of a percent.

_____

LESSON 8-2
Percents, Fractions, and Decimals
Reteach

To change a decimal to a percent:
- move the decimal point two places to the right;
- write the % symbol after the number.

$$0.07 = .07. = 7\%$$

Write each decimal as a percent.

1. 0.34

2. 0.06

3. 0.93

4. 0.57

_____ _____ _____ _____

5. 0.8

6. 0.734

7. 0.082

8. 0.225

_____ _____ _____ _____

9. 0.604

10. 0.09

11. 0.518

12. 1.03

_____ _____ _____ _____

To change a fraction to a percent:
- Find an equivalent fraction with a denominator of 100.
- Use the numerator of the equivalent fraction as the percent.

$$\frac{8}{25} = \frac{x}{100}$$

$$\frac{8 \cdot 4}{25 \cdot 4} = \frac{32}{100}$$

$$\frac{8}{25} = \frac{32}{100} = 32\%$$

Think: $100 \div 25 = 4$. So, multiply the numerator and denominator by 4.

Write each fraction as a percent.

13. $\frac{3}{10}$

14. $\frac{2}{50}$

15. $\frac{7}{20}$

16. $\frac{1}{5}$

_____ _____ _____ _____

17. $\frac{1}{8}$

18. $\frac{3}{25}$

19. $\frac{3}{4}$

20. $\frac{23}{50}$

_____ _____ _____ _____

21. $\frac{11}{20}$

22. $\frac{43}{50}$

23. $\frac{24}{25}$

24. $\frac{7}{8}$

_____ _____ _____ _____

LESSON 8-3 Solving Percent Problems

Practice and Problem Solving: A/B

Solve.

1. 22 students is ____% of 55.

2. 24 red marbles is 40% of ____ marbles.

3. 15% of $9 is $_____.

4. 12 is ____ % of 200.

5. Yesterday, Bethany sent 60 text messages. She said that 15% of those messages were to her best friend. How many text messages did Bethany send to her friend yesterday?

_____

6. In a survey, 27% of the people chose salads over a meat dish. In all, 81 people chose salads. How many people were in the survey?

_____

7. The sales tax on a $350 computer is $22.75. Find the sales tax rate.

_____

Use the circle graph to complete Exercises 8–11.

8. If 6,000 people voted in the election, how many were from 18 to 29 years old?

_____

9. If 12,000 people voted in the election, how many were from 50 to 64 years old?

_____

10. If 596 people voted in the election, how many were over 65 years old?

_____

11. Suppose that Sahil knows that 45 people with ages of 18 to 29 voted. Without using a calculator, he quickly says then 135 people with ages of 30 to 49 voted. Is he correct? How might Sahil have come up with his answer so quickly?

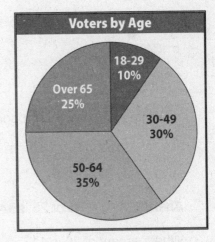

Voters by Age

18-29 10%
30-49 30%
50-64 35%
Over 65 25%

_____

_____

_____

Solving Percent Problems

LESSON 8-3

Reteach

You can use this proportion to solve percent problems.

$$\frac{part}{total} = \frac{percent}{100}$$

9 is what percent of 12?

Think: part   unknown   total

> The number following "of" is the total.

30% of what number is 24?

Think: percent   unknown   part

$$\frac{9}{12} = \frac{x}{100}$$

$12 \cdot x = 9 \cdot 100$

$12x = 900$

$$\frac{12x}{12} = \frac{900}{12}$$

$x = 75$

So, 9 is 75% of 12.

$$\frac{24}{x} = \frac{30}{100}$$

$30 \cdot x = 24 \cdot 100$

$30x = 2,400$

$$\frac{30x}{30} = \frac{2,400}{30}$$

$x = 80$

So, 30% of 80 is 24.

Solve.

1. What percent of 25 is 14?

   a. part = _____

   b. total = _____

   c. percent = _____

   d. Write and solve the proportion.

2. 80% of what number is 16?

   a. part = _____

   b. total = _____

   c. percent = _____

   d. Write and solve the proportion.

   Answer: _____ % of 25 is 14.

   Answer: 80% of _____ is 16.

3. What percent of 20 is 11? _____

4. 18 is 45% of what number? _____

5. 15 is what percent of 5? _____

6. 75% of what number is 105? _____

LESSON 9-1 Exponents

Practice and Problem Solving: A/B

Write each expression in exponential form and find its value.

1. $2 \times 2 \times 2 \times 2$

2. $3 \times 3 \times 3$

3. $\dfrac{3}{5} \times \dfrac{3}{5}$

_____

_____

_____

4. 10×10

5. $\dfrac{1}{6} \times \dfrac{1}{6} \times \dfrac{1}{6} \times \dfrac{1}{6}$

6. $0.5 \times 0.5 \times 0.5$

_____

_____

_____

Find each value.

7. $(1.2)^3$

8. $\left(\dfrac{1}{4}\right)^4$

9. $(2)^6$

10. 2^6

_____

_____

_____

_____

Solve.

11. The volume of a cubic box is 10^6 cubic millimeters.
Write the volume of the box in standard form.

_____

How long is each side of the box? (*Hint*: The length, width, and height of a cube are equal.)

_____

12. The voltage in an electrical circuit is multiplied by itself each time it is

reduced. The voltage is $\dfrac{27}{125}$ of a volt and it has been reduced three

times. Write the voltage in exponential form. _____

What was the original voltage in the circuit? _____

Compare using >, <, or =.

13. $\left(\dfrac{1}{3}\right)^4$ _____ $\left(\dfrac{1}{3}\right)^0$

14. $(1)^5$ _____ 1^5

15. 5^0 _____ -5^0

16. Use exponents to write 81 three different ways.

81 = _____ ; 81 = _____ ; 81 = _____

LESSON 9-1

Exponents

Reteach

You can write a number in exponential form to show repeated multiplication. A number written in exponential form has a **base** and an **exponent**. The exponent tells you how many times a number, the base, is used as a factor.

$8^4 \longleftarrow$ exponent

base

Write the expression in exponential form.

$(0.7) \times (0.7) \times (0.7) \times (0.7)$

0.7 is used as a factor 4 times.

$(0.7) \times (0.7) \times (0.7) \times (0.7) = (0.7)^4$

Write each expression in exponential form.

1. $\dfrac{1}{20} \times \dfrac{1}{20} \times \dfrac{1}{20} \times \dfrac{1}{20}$
2. 8×8
3. $7.5 \times 7.5 \times 7.5$
4. (0.4)

_____ _____ _____ _____

You can find the value of expressions in exponential form.
Find the value.
5^6

Step 1 Write the expression as repeated multiplication.
$5 \times 5 \times 5 \times 5 \times 5 \times 5$

Step 2 Multiply.
$5 \times 5 \times 5 \times 5 \times 5 \times 5 = 15{,}625$

$5^6 = 15{,}625$

Simplify.

5. $\left(\dfrac{1}{2}\right)^3$
6. $(1.2)^5$
7. 3^6
8. $\left(\dfrac{4}{3}\right)^2$

_____ _____ _____ _____

LESSON 9-2

Prime Factorization

Practice and Problem Solving: A/B

Fill in the missing information. Add more "steps" to the ladder diagram and more "branches" to the tree diagram, if needed. Then, write the prime factorization of each number.

1.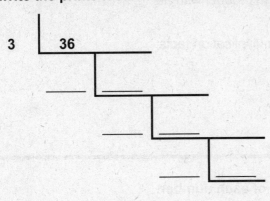

2.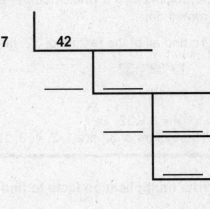

_____

3. 48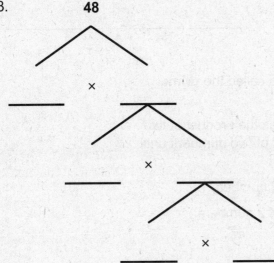

4. 27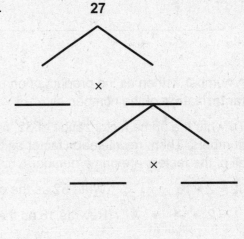

_____

Write the prime factorizations.

5. 44

6. 125

7. 85

8. 39

_____ _____ _____ _____

LESSON 9-2

Prime Factorization
Reteach

Factors of a product are the numbers that are multiplied to give that product.

A factor is also a whole number that divides the product with no remainder.

To find all of the factors of 32, make a list of multiplication facts.

$1 \bullet 32 = 32$

$2 \bullet 16 = 32$

$4 \bullet 8 = 32$

The factors of 32 are 1, 2, 4, 8, 16, and 32.

Write multiplication facts to find the factors of each number.

1. 28

2. 15

_____

3. 36

4. 29

_____

A number written as the product of prime factors is called the **prime factorization** of the number.

To write the prime factorization of 32, first write it as the product of two numbers. Then, rewrite each factor as the product of two numbers until all of the factors are prime numbers.

$32 = 2 \bullet \mathbf{16}$ (Write 32 as the product of 2 numbers.)

$= 2 \bullet \mathbf{4} \bullet \mathbf{4}$ (Rewrite 16 as the product of 2 numbers.)

      ↓   ↓

$= 2 \bullet 2 \bullet 2 \bullet 2 \bullet 2$ (Rewrite the 4's as the product 2 prime numbers.)

So, the prime factorization of 32 is $2 \bullet 2 \bullet 2 \bullet 2 \bullet 2$ or 2^5.

Find the prime factorization of each number.

5. 28

6. 45

7. 50

8. 72

_____   _____   _____   _____

LESSON 9-3 Order of Operations

Practice and Problem Solving: A/B

Name the operation you should perform first.

1. $4 \times 6 - 3$

2. $1 + 8 \div 2$

3. $(2 + 5) - 4^2$

_____

_____

_____

4. $7 \div 7^3 \times 7$

5. $8^2 \div (8 - 4)^2$

6. $-4 + 3^3 \div 5$

_____

_____

_____

Match each expression to its value.

Expression	Value
7. $7 + 8 - 2$	A. 9
8. $9 + (12 - 10)$	B. 40
9. $(20 - 15) \times 2$	C. 12
10. $10 \div 5 + 7$	D. 14
11. $6 + 2 \times 3$	E. 16
12. $(2 \times 4) + 8$	F. 11
13. $14 + 2 \times 0$	G. 13
14. $(5 - 1) \times 10$	H. 10

15. A sixth-grade student bought three cans of tennis balls for $4 each. Sales tax for all three cans was $.95. Write an expression to show the total amount the student paid.

_____

16. The middle-school camera club sold 240 tulip bulbs and 360 daffodil bulbs. Students divided the bulbs into 100 bags to sell at the school fair. Write an expression to show how many bulbs went into each of the 100 bags if students put the same number of each kind of bulb in each bag.

_____

LESSON 9-3	# Order of Operations

Reteach

A mathematical phrase that includes only numbers and operations is called a *numerical expression*.

$9 + 8 \times 3 \div 6$ is a numerical expression.

When you evaluate a numerical expression, you find its value.

You can use the order of operations to evaluate a numerical expression.

<u>Order of operations:</u>

1. Do all operations within *parentheses*.
2. Find the values of numbers with *exponents*.
3. *Multiply* and *divide* in order from left to right.
4. *Add* and *subtract* in order from left to right.

Evaluate the expression.

$60 \div (7 + 3) + 3^2$

$60 \div 10 + 3^2$	Do all operations within parentheses.
$60 \div 10 + 9$	Find the values of numbers with exponents.
$6 + 9$	Multiply and divide in order from left to right.
15	Add and subtract in order from left to right.

Evaluate each numerical expression.

1. $7 \times (12 + 8) - 6$

    $7 \times$ _____ $- 6$

    _____ $- 6$

    _____

2. $10 \times (12 + 34) + 3$

    $10 \times$ _____ $+ 3$

    _____ $+ 3$

    _____

3. $10 + (6 \times 5) - 7$

    $10 +$ _____ $- 7$

    _____ $- 7$

    _____

4. $2^3 + (10 - 4)$

5. $7 + 3 \times (8 + 5)$

6. $36 \div 4 + 11 \times 8$

7. $5^2 - (2 \times 8) + 9$

8. $3 \times (12 \div 4) - 2^2$

9. $(3^3 + 10) - 2$

Solve.

10. Write and evaluate your own numerical expression. Use parentheses, exponents, and at least two operations.

_____

Name _____ Date _____ Class_____

Modeling and Writing Expressions

Practice and Problem Solving: A/B

Solve.

1. Jessica rode 9 miles farther than Roger rode. Let r represent the number of miles Roger rode. Write an expression for the number of miles Jessica rode.

   _____

2. Let m represent the number of children playing soccer. Those children are separated into 4 equal teams. Write an expression for the number of children on each team.

   _____

3. Glenda bought some apps for her tablet. Each app cost \$5. Let n represent the number of apps she bought. Write an expression to show the total amount she spent.

   _____

Write each phrase as a numerical or algebraic expression.

4. 25 multiplied by 3

   _____

5. 3 added to n

   _____

6. r divided by 8

   _____

7. the product of 7 and m

   _____

8. the difference between 48 and 13

   _____

9. the quotient of 18 and 3

   _____

10. 189 subtracted from t

   _____

11. the sum of w and 253

   _____

Write two word phrases for each expression.

12. $t + 23$ _____

13. $45 - n$ _____

Solve.

14. Write an expression that has two terms. Your expression should have a variable and a constant.

   _____

Modeling and Writing Expressions
Reteach

Write an expression that shows how much longer the Nile River is than
the Amazon River.

NILE RIVER

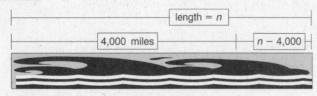

The expression is **$n - 4{,}000$**.

AMAZON RIVER

Each state gets the same number of senators. Write an expression for
the number of senators there are in the United States Congress.

There are
50 states.

There are *s*
senators from
each state.

50s

The total number of
senators is **50 times *s***.

Solve.

1. Why does the first problem above use subtraction?

   _____

2. Why does the second problem above use multiplication?

   _____

3. Jackson had *n* autographs in his autograph book. Yesterday he got 3
   more autographs. Write an expression to show how many autographs
   are in his autograph book now.

   _____

4. Miranda earned $*c* for working 8 hours. Write an expression to show
   how much Miranda earned for each hour worked.

   _____

LESSON 10-2 Evaluating Expressions

Practice and Problem Solving: A/B

Evaluate each expression for the given value(s) of the variable(s).

1. $a - 4$ when $a = 16$

2. $2b + 9$ when $b = 3$

_____

_____

3. $c \div 2$ when $c = 26$

4. $5(9 + d) - 6$ when $d = 3$

_____

_____

5. $g^2 + 23$ when $g = 6$

6. $3h - j$ when $h = 8$ and $j = 11$

_____

_____

7. $(n - 2) \bullet m$ when $n = 5$ and $m = 9$

8. $r(s^2)(t)$ when $r = 2$, $s = 3$, and $t = 5$

_____

_____

Use the given values to complete each table.

9.

p	$2(13 - p)$
2	
3	
4	

10.

v	w	$3v + w$
4	2	
6	3	
8	4	

11.

x	y	$x^2 \div y$
2	1	
6	2	
8	4	

Solve.

12. The sales tax in one town is 8%. So, the total cost of an item can be written as $c + 0.08c$. What is the total cost of an item that sells for $12?

_____

13. To change knots per hour to miles per hour, use the expression $1.15k$, where k is the speed in knots per hour. A plane is flying at 300 knots per hour. How fast is that plane flying in miles per hour?

_____

14. Lurinda ordered some boxes of greeting cards online. The cost of the cards is $6.50n + $3 where n is the number of boxes ordered and $3 is the shipping and handling charge. How much will Lurinda pay if she orders 8 boxes of cards?

_____

LESSON
10-2
Evaluating Expressions
Reteach

A **variable** is a letter that represents a number that can change in an expression. When you **evaluate** an algebraic expression, you substitute the value given for the variable in the expression.

- Algebraic expression: $x - 3$

  The value of the expression depends on the value of the variable x.

  If $x = 7$ → $7 - 3 = 4$

  If $x = 11$ → $11 - 3 = 8$

  If $x = 25$ → $25 - 3 = 22$

- Evaluate $4n + 5$ for $n = 7$.

  Replace the variable n with 7. → $4(7) + 5$

  Evaluate, following the order of operations. → $4(7) + 5 = 28 + 5 = 33$

Evaluate each expression for the given value. Show your work.

1. $a + 7$ when $a = 3$

   $a + 7 = 3 + 7 =$ ____

2. $y \div 3$ when $y = 6$

   $y \div 3 =$ ____ $\div 3 =$ ____

3. $n - 5$ when $n = 15$

   $n - 5 =$ ____ $- 5 =$ ____

4. $(6 + d) \bullet 2$ when $d = 3$

   $(6 + d) \bullet 2 = (6 +$ ____ $) \bullet 2$

   $=$ _____ $\bullet 2 =$ ____

5. $3n - 2$ when $n = 5$

   $3n - 2 = 3($ ____ $) - 2 =$ ____

6. $6b$ when $b = 7$

   _____

7. $12 - f$ when $f = 3$

   _____

8. $\dfrac{m}{5}$ when $m = 35$

   _____

9. $2k + 5$ when $k = 8$

   _____

10. $10 - (p + 3)$ when $p = 7$

    _____

LESSON 10-3 **Generating Equivalent Expressions**

Practice and Problem Solving: A/B

Justify each step used to simplify the expression.

1. $3x + 2y - 2x + 2 = 3x - 2x + 2y + 2$ _____

2. $\qquad = (3x - 2x) + 2y + 2$ _____

3. $\qquad = (3 - 2)x + 2y + 2$ _____

4. $\qquad = x + 2y + 2$ _____

Simplify.

5. $3r + n^2 - r + 5 - 2n + 2$ _____

6. $8v + w + 7 - 8v + 2w$ _____

7. $4c^2 + 6c - 3c^2 - 2c - 3$ _____

8. $z^3 + 5z + 3z^2 + 1 - 4 - 2z^2$ _____

Write and simplify an expression for the perimeter of each figure.

9.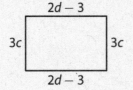

10.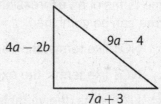

_____   _____

11. A square has sides of $10x$. Write and simplify an expression for the perimeter of that square.

_____

12. A rectangle has a length of $2x + 7$ and a width of $3x + 8y$. Write and simplify an expression for the perimeter of that rectangle.

_____

13. In the space at the right, draw a triangle. Use an algebraic expression to label the length of each side. Write an expression for the perimeter of your triangle. Then simplify that expression.

_____

LESSON 10-3 Generating Equivalent Expressions
Reteach

Look at the following expressions: $x = 1x$

$$x + x = 2x$$
$$x + x + x = 3x$$

The numbers 1, 2, and 3 are called **coefficients** of x.

Identify each coefficient.

1. $8x$ ____

2. $3m$ ____

3. y ____

4. $14t$ ____

An algebraic expression has terms that are separated by + and −.
In the expression $2x + 5y$, the **terms** are $2x$ and $5y$.

Expression	Terms
$8x + 4y$	$8x$ and $4y$
$5m - 2m + 9$	$5m$, $-2m$, and 9
$4a^2 - 2b + c - 2a^2$	$4a^2$, $-2b$, c, and $-2a^2$

Sometimes the terms of an expression can be combined.
Only **like terms** can be combined.

$2x + 2y$ NOT like terms, the variables are different.

$4a^2 - 2a$ NOT like terms, the exponents are different.

$5m - 2m$ Like terms, the variables and exponents are both the same.

$n^3 + 2n^3$ Like terms, the variables and exponents are both the same.

To **simplify** an expression, combine like terms by adding or subtracting
the coefficients of the variable.

$$5m - 2m = 3m$$

$4a^2 + 5a + a + 3 = 4a^2 + 6a + 3$ Note that the coefficient of a is 1.

Simplify.

5. $8x + 2x$

6. $3m - m$

7. $6y + 6y$

8. $14t - 3t$

_____

_____

_____

_____

9. $3b + b + 6$

10. $9a - 3a + 4$

11. $n + 5n - 3c$

12. $12d - 2d + e$

_____

_____

_____

_____

LESSON 11-1

Writing Equations to Represent Situations

Practice and Problem Solving: A/B

Determine whether the given value is a solution of the equation. Write *yes* or *no*.

1. $x + 11 = 15$; $x = 4$ _____

2. $36 - w = 10$; $w = 20$ _____

3. $0.2v = 1.2$; $v = 10$ _____

4. $15 = 6 + d$; $d = 8$ _____

5. $28 - w = 25$; $w = 3$ _____

6. $4t = 32$; $t = 8$ _____

7. $\dfrac{12}{s} = 4$; $s = 3$ _____

8. $\dfrac{33}{p} = 3$; $p = 11$ _____

Circle the letter of the equation that each given solution makes true.

9. $m = 19$

   A $10 + m = 20$ C $7m = 26$

   B $m - 4 = 15$ D $\dfrac{18}{m} = 2$

10. $a = 16$

   A $2a = 18$ C $24 - a = 6$

   B $a + 12 = 24$ D $\dfrac{a}{4} = 4$

Write an equation to represent each situation.

11. Seventy-two people signed up for the soccer league. After the players were evenly divided into teams, there were 6 teams in the league and x people on each team.

_____

12. Mary covered her kitchen floor with 10 tiles. The floor measures 6 feet long by 5 feet wide. The tiles are each 3 feet long and w feet wide.

_____

Solve.

13. The low temperature was 35°F. This was 13°F lower than the daytime high temperature. Write an equation to determine whether the high temperature was 48°F or 42°F.

_____

14. Kayla bought 16 bagels. She paid a total of $20. Write an equation to determine whether each bagel cost $1.50 or $1.25.

_____

15. Write a real-world situation that could be modeled by the equation $\dfrac{24}{y} = 3$. Then solve the problem.

_____

_____

_____

LESSON 11-1

Writing Equations to Represent Situations
Reteach

An **equation** is a mathematical sentence that says that two quantities are equal.

Some equations contain variables. A **solution** for an equation is a value for a variable that makes the statement true.

You can write related facts using addition and subtraction.
$7 + 6 = 13$ $13 - 6 = 7$

You can write related facts using multiplication and division.
$3 \cdot 4 = 12$ $\dfrac{12}{4} = 3$

You can use related facts to find solutions for equations. If the related fact matches the value for the variable, then that value is a solution.

A. $x + 5 = 9$; $x = 3$

Think: $9 - 5 = x$
$4 = x$
$4 \neq 3$

3 is **not** a solution of $x + 5 = 9$.

B. $x - 7 = 5$; $x = 12$

Think: $5 + 7 = x$
$12 = x$
$12 = 12$

12 is a solution of $x - 7 = 5$.

C. $2x = 14$; $x = 9$

Think: $14 \div 2 = x$
$7 = x$
$7 \neq 9$

9 is **not** a solution of $2x = 14$.

D. $\dfrac{x}{5} = 3$; $x = 15$

Think: $3 \cdot 5 = x$
$15 = x$
$15 = 15$

15 is a solution of $x \div 5 = 3$.

Use related facts to determine whether the given value is a solution for each equation.

1. $x + 6 = 14$; $x = 8$

2. $\dfrac{s}{4} = 5$; $s = 24$

3. $g - 3 = 7$; $g = 11$

_____

4. $3a = 18$; $a = 6$

5. $26 = y - 9$; $y = 35$

6. $b \cdot 5 = 20$; $b = 3$

_____

7. $15 = \dfrac{v}{3}$; $v = 45$

8. $11 = p + 6$; $p = 5$

9. $6k = 78$; $k = 12$

_____

LESSON 11-2

Addition and Subtraction Equations

Practice and Problem Solving: A/B

Solve each equation. Graph the solution on the number line.

1. $6 = r + 2$ $r =$ ____

2. $26 = w - 12$ $w =$ ____

3. $\dfrac{1}{2} = m - \dfrac{1}{8}$ $m =$ ____

4. $t + 1 = -3$ $t =$ ____

Use the drawing at the right for Exercises 5–6.

5. Write an equation to represent the measures of the angles.

   _____

6. Solve the equation to find the measure of the unknown angle.

   _____

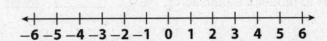

Use the drawing at the right for Exercises 7–8.

7. Write an equation to represent the measures of the angles.

   _____

8. Solve the equation to find the measure of the unknown angle.

   _____

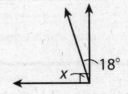

Write a problem for the equation $3 + x = 8$. Then solve the equation and write the answer to your problem.

9. _____

   _____

   _____

Addition and Subtraction Equations

Reteach

To solve an equation, you need to get the variable alone on one side of the equal sign.

You can use tiles to help you solve subtraction equations.

Variable   add 1   subtract 1

Addition undoes subtraction, so you can use addition to solve subtraction equations.

One positive tile and one negative tile make a **zero pair**.

Zero pair: $+1 + (-1) = 0$

add 1

subtract 1

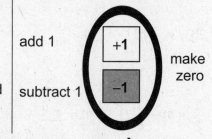

make zero

To solve $x - 4 = 2$, first use tiles to model the equation.

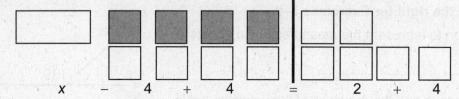

X $-$ 4 $=$ 2

To get the variable alone, you have to add positive tiles. Remember to add the same number of positive tiles to each side of the equation.

x $-$ 4 $+$ 4 $=$ 2 $+$ 4

Then remove the greatest possible number of zero pairs from each side of the equal sign.

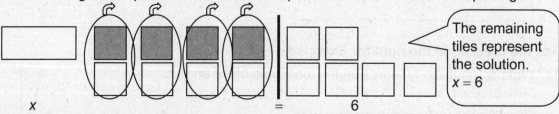

x $=$ 6

The remaining tiles represent the solution. $x = 6$

Use tiles to solve each equation.

1. $x - 5 = 3$

   $x =$ ____

2. $x - 2 = 7$

   $x =$ ____

3. $x - 1 = 4$

   $x =$ ____

4. $x - 8 = 1$

   $x =$ ____

5. $x - 3 = 3$

   $x =$ ____

6. $x - 6 = 2$

   $x =$ ____

| **LESSON** | **Multiplication and Division Equations** |
| **11-3** | *Practice and Problem Solving: A/B* |

Solve each equation. Graph the solution on the number line. Check your work.

1. $\dfrac{e}{2} = 3$ $e =$ _____

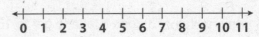

_____

_____

2. $20 = 2w$ $w =$ _____

_____

_____

3. $\dfrac{1}{2} = 2m$ $m =$ _____

_____

_____

4. $\dfrac{k}{5} = 2$ $k =$ _____

_____

_____

Use the drawing at the right for Exercises 5–6.

5. Write an equation you can use to find the length of the rectangle.

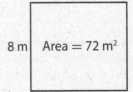

8 m | Area = 72 m²

x m

_____

6. Solve the equation. Give the length of the rectangle.

_____

Solve.

7. Alise separated her pictures into 3 piles. Each pile contained 9 pictures. How many pictures did she have in all? Write and solve an equation to represent the problem. State the answer to the problem.

_____

_____

LESSON
11-3

Multiplication and Division Equations
Reteach

Number lines can be used to solve multiplication and division equations.

Solve: $3n = 15$

How many moves of 3 does it take to get to 15?

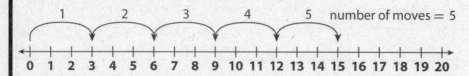

$n = 5$ Check: $3 \cdot 5 = 15$✓

Solve: $\dfrac{n}{3} = 4$

If you make 3 moves of 4, where are you on the number line?

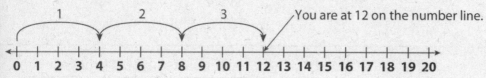

You are at 12 on the number line.

$n = 12$ Check: $12 \div 3 = 4$✓

Show the moves you can use to solve each equation. Then give the solution to the equation and check your work.

1. $3n = 9$

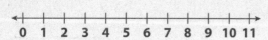

Solution: $n =$ ____

Show your check:

2. $\dfrac{n}{2} = 4$

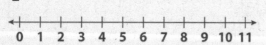

Solution: $n =$ ____

Show your check:

LESSON
11-4

Writing Inequalities

Practice and Problem Solving: A/B

Complete the graph for each inequality.

1. $a > 3$

2. $r \le -2$

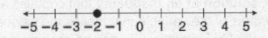

Graph the solutions of each inequality. Check the solutions.

3. $w \ge 0$

 Check: _____

4. $b \le -4$

 Check: _____

5. $a < 1.5$

 Check: _____

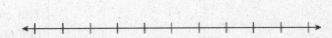

Write an inequality that represents each phrase. Draw a graph to represent the inequality.

6. The sum of 1 and x is less than 5.

 _____

7. 3 is less than y minus 2.

 _____

Write and graph an inequality to represent each situation.

8. The temperature today will be at least 10°F. _____

9. Ben wants to spend no more than $3. _____

Write an inequality that matches the number line model.

10. _____

11. _____

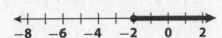

LESSON 11-4

Writing Inequalities
Reteach

An equation is a statement that says two quantities are equal. An **inequality** is a statement that says two quantities are **not** equal.

A **solution of an inequality** that contains a variable is any value or values of the variable that makes the inequality true. All values that make the inequality true can be shown on a graph.

Inequality	Meaning	Solution of Inequality
$x > 3$	All numbers *greater than* 3	![number line] $-5\ -4\ -3\ -2\ -1\ 0\ 1\ 2\ 3\ 4\ 5$ The *open circle* at 3 shows that the value 3 is **not** included in the solution.
$x \geq 3$	All numbers *greater than or equal to* 3	![number line] $-5\ -4\ -3\ -2\ -1\ 0\ 1\ 2\ 3\ 4\ 5$ The *closed circle* at 3 shows that the value 3 **is** included in the solution.
$x < 3$	All numbers *less than* 3	![number line] $-5\ -4\ -3\ -2\ -1\ 0\ 1\ 2\ 3\ 4\ 5$
$x \leq 3$	All numbers *less than or equal to* 3	![number line] $-5\ -4\ -3\ -2\ -1\ 0\ 1\ 2\ 3\ 4\ 5$

Graph the solutions of each inequality.

1. $x > -4$

• Draw an open circle at –4.

• Read $x > -4$ as "x is greater than –4."

• Draw an arrow to the right of –4.

$-5\ -4\ -3\ -2\ -1\ 0\ 1\ 2\ 3\ 4\ 5$

2. $x \leq 1$

• Draw a closed circle at 1.

• Read $x \leq 1$ as "x is less than or equal to 1."

• Draw an arrow to the left of 1.

$-5\ -4\ -3\ -2\ -1\ 0\ 1\ 2\ 3\ 4\ 5$

3. $a > -1$

$-5\ -4\ -3\ -2\ -1\ 0\ 1\ 2\ 3\ 4\ 5$

4. $y \leq 3$

$-5\ -4\ -3\ -2\ -1\ 0\ 1\ 2\ 3\ 4\ 5$

Write an inequality that represents each phrase.

5. The sum of 2 and 3 is less than *y*.

_____

6. The sum of *y* and 2 is greater than or equal to 6.

_____

LESSON 12-1

Graphing on the Coordinate Plane
Practice and Problem Solving: A/B

Give the coordinates of the points on the coordinate plane.

1. A (____ , ____)

2. B (____ , ____)

3. C (____ , ____)

4. D (____ , ____)

5. E (____ , ____)

6. F (____ , ____)

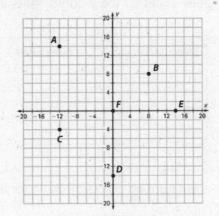

Plot the points on the coordinate plane.

7. G (2, 4)

8. H (–6, 8)

9. J (10, –12)

10. K (–14, –16)

11. M (0, 18)

12. P (–20, 0)

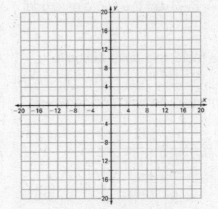

Describe how to go from one store to the next on the map. Use words like *left*, *right*, *up*, *down*, *north*, *south*, *east*, and *west*. Each square on the coordinate plane is a city block.

13. The computer store, A, to the food store, B.

_____

14. The computer store, A, to the hardware store, C.

_____

15. The hardware store, C, to the food store, B.

_____

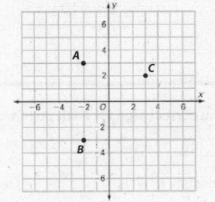

<table>
<tr><td>**LESSON**
12-1</td><td colspan="2"># Graphing on the Coordinate Plane
Reteach</td></tr>
</table>

Each quadrant of the coordinate plane has a unique combination of positive and negative signs for the *x*-coordinates and *y*-coordinates as shown here.

Quadrant	*x*-coordinate	*y*-coordinate
I	+	+
II	−	+
III	−	−
IV	+	−

Use these rules when naming points on the coordinate plane.

Example 1

Draw the point *A*(1, −3) on the coordinate grid.

Solution

According to the table, this point will be in Quadrant IV.

So, go to the *right* (+) one unit, and go *down* (−) three units.

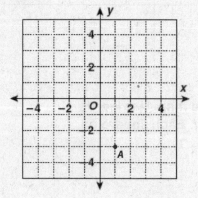

Example 2

What are the coordinates of point *B*?

Solution

According to the table, this point will have a negative *x*-coordinate and a positive *y*-coordinate.

Point *B* is 3 three units to the *left* (−) and four units *up* (+). So the coordinates of point *B* are (−3, 4).

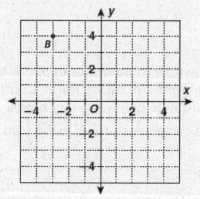

Add the correct sign for each point's coordinates.

1. (___ 3, ___ 4) in

   Quadrant II

2. (___ 2, ___ 5) in

   Quadrant IV

3. (___ 9, ___ 1) in

   Quadrant I

4. In which quadrant is the point (0, 7) located? Explain your answer.

_____

LESSON 12-2

Independent and Dependent Variables in Tables and Graphs
Practice and Problem Solving: A/B

Name the *dependent variable* and the *independent variable* in each problem.

1. A food service worker earns $12 per hour. How much money, *m*, does the worker earn on a shift of *h* hours?

   Dependent variable: _____; independent variable: _____

2. A large 2-topping pizza, *L*, costs $2 more than a medium 3-topping pizza, *M*.

   Dependent variable: _____; independent variable: _____

The table shows the electric current produced by a solar cell in different amounts of sunlight (light intensity). Answer the questions using the data.

Light intensity	150	300	450	600	750	900
Current	10	30	45	60	75	90

3. What is the dependent variable?

   _____

4. What is the independent variable?

   _____

5. What do you predict the current will be in the absence of sunlight? Explain.

   _____

6. What do you predict the current will be if the light intensity is 1,000? Explain.

   _____

A race car driver's time in seconds to complete 12 laps is plotted on the graph.

7. Which axis shows the dependent variable?

   _____

8. Why does the graph begin at *x* = 1?

   _____

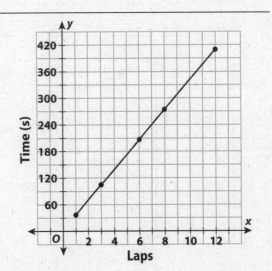

**LESSON
12-2**
Independent and Dependent Variables in Tables and Graphs
Reteach

In a table, the *independent variable* is often represented by *x*. The *dependent variable* is often represented by *y*. Look at this example.

x	0	1	2	3	4	5	6	7
y	4	5	6	7	8	9	10	?

What *y* value goes for the question mark?

Step 1 Notice that 4 is added to each value of *x* to give the *y* value.

Step 2 So, add 4 to 7. What does this give? $4 + 7 = 11$

On a chart or graph,

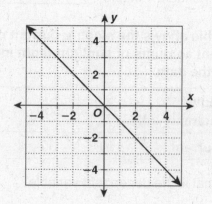

- the *x*-axis is usually used for the *independent variable*, and

- the *y*-axis is usually used for the *dependent variable*.

Look at the example. ⟶

How does *y* depend on *x*?

Step 1 Each value of *y* is the opposite of the value of *x*.

Step 2 What equation shows this fact?
$y = -x$

Give the relationship between x and y.

1.

x	1	2	3	4	5
y	3	4	5	6	7

_____

2.

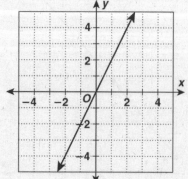

a. What is *y* when $x = 2$?

_____

b. What value of *x* gives $y = -2$?

_____

c. Write the equation for the graph.

_____

Writing Equations from Tables

Practice and Problem Solving: A/B

Write an equation to express y in terms of x. Use your equation to complete the table.

1.

x	1	2	3	4	5
y	7	14	21	28	

_____

2.

x	2	3	4	5	6
y	−3	−2	−1	0	

_____

3.

x	20	16	12	8	4
y	10	8	6	4	

_____

4.

x	7	8	9	10	11
y	11	12	13	14	

_____

Solve.

5. Henry records how many days he rides his bike and how far he rides each week. He rides the same distance each time. He rode 18 miles in 3 days, 24 miles in 4 days, and 42 miles in 7 days. Write and solve an equation to find how far he rides his bike in 10 days.

Number of days, d	3	4	7	10
Number of miles, m	18			

Equation relating d and m is _____.

The number of miles Henry rides his bike in 10 days is _____.

6. When Cabrini is 6, Nikos is 2. When Cabrini is 10, Nikos will be 6. When Cabrini is 16, Nikos will be 12. When Cabrini is 21, Nikos will be 17. Write and solve an equation to find Nikos' age when Cabrini is 40.

Cabrini's age, x	6	10	16	21	40
Nikos' age, y	2				

Equation relating x and y is _____.

When Cabrini is 40 years old, Nikos will be _____.

LESSON
12-3

Writing Equations from Tables
Reteach

The relationship between two variables in which one quantity depends on the other can be modeled by an equation. The equation expresses the dependent variable *y* in terms of the independent variable *x*.

x	0	1	2	3	4	5	6	7
y	4	5	6	7	8	9	10	?

To write an equation from a table of values, first compare the *x*- and *y*-values to find a pattern. In each, the *y*-value is 4 more than the *x*-value.

Then use the pattern to write an equation expressing *y* in terms of *x*.
$y = x + 4$

You can use the equation to find the missing value in the table.
To find *y* when $x = 7$, substitute 7 in for *x* in the equation.

$y = x + 4$
$y = 7 + 4$
$y = 11$
So, *y* is **11** when *x* is 7.

Write an equation to express *y* in terms of *x*. Use your equation to find the missing value of *y*.

1.

x	1	2	3	4	5	6
y	3	6	9	12	15	?

_____

2.

x	18	17	16	15	14	13
y	15	14	13	?	11	10

_____

To solve a real-world problem, use a table of values and an equation.

When Todd is 8, Jane is 1. When Todd is 10, Jane will be 3. When Todd is 16, Jane will be 9. What is Jane's age when Todd is 45?

Todd, *x*	8	10	16	45
Jane, *y*	1	3	9	?

Jane is 7 years younger than Todd.
So $y = x - 7$. When $x = 45$, $y = 45 - 7$. So, $y = 38$.

Solve.

3. When a rectangle is 3 inches wide its length is 6 inches. When it is 4 inches wide its length will be 8 inches. When it is is 9 inches wide its length will be 18 inches. Write and solve an equation to complete the table.

Width, *x*	3	4	9	20
Length, *y*	6			

_____

When the rectangle is 20 inches wide, its length is _____.

LESSON 12-4 Representing Algebraic Relationships in Tables and Graphs

Practice and Problem Solving: A/B

An antiques dealer has 24 clock radios to sell at a 12-hour-long antique-radio sale. Use the graph to complete the table.

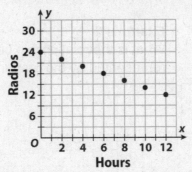

1. Complete the table with the data from the graph.

Radios remaining	24	?	?	?	?	?	?
Hours completed	0	2	4	6	8	10	12

2. What are the dependent (*y*) and independent (*x*) variables?

   dependent: _____; independent: _____

3. Write ordered pairs for the points on the graph and in the table.

   _____

4. How many radios are sold every two hours? _____

5. What happens to the *total* number of radios every two hours?

   _____

6. If *h* is hours and *n* is the number of radios remaining, complete the equation:

   $n =$ _____ $\times h +$ _____

7. Why is the sign of the number that is multiplied by hours, *h*, negative?

   _____

LESSON
12-4

Representing Algebraic Relationships in Tables and Graphs
Reteach

The *x*- and *y*-values in an algebraic relationship should be related in the same way when new values of *x* or *y* are used. This pattern should be seen in a table of values and from a graph of the *x* and *y* values.

Example 1

What is the relationship of the *x* and *y* values in the table?

x	2	4	6	8	10
y	6	12	18	24	30

Solution

First, check to see if there is a simple addition, multiplication, division, or subtraction relationship between the *x* and *y* values.

Here, the *y* values are 3 times the *x* values.

This means that the algebraic relationship is $y = 3x$.

Example 2

What is the relationship between *x* and *y* represented by the graph.

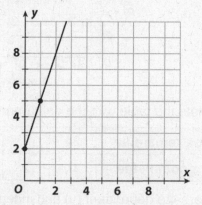

Solution

First, notice that the line through the points crosses the *y*-axis at $y = 2$. This means that part of the relationship between *x* and *y* is given by $y = \underline{\quad} + 2$.

Next, notice that the line through the points goes over to the right by one unit as it "rises" by 3 units. This means that any *x* value is multiplied by 3 over 1 or 3 units as the line goes from one point to another. This is written as $y = 3x$.

Combine these two observations:
$y = 3x$ and $y = 2$ give $y = 3x + 2$.
Both parts are needed to completely describe the relationship shown.

---

1. Find the relationship of *x* and *y* in the table.

x	0	1	3	6	7
y	1.5	2	3	4.5	5

$y = $ _____ *x* + _____

2. Find the relationship of *x* and *y* from a graph of a line that crosses the *y*-axis at $y = 6$ and that goes to the left 2 units and rises 3 units.

$y = $ _____ *x* + _____

LESSON 13-1

Area of Quadrilaterals

Practice and Problem Solving: A/B

Find the area of each parallelogram.

1.

18 ft
16 ft

_____

2.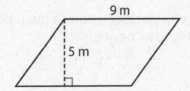

9 m
5 m

_____

Find the area of each trapezoid.

3.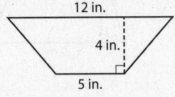

12 in.
4 in.
5 in.

_____

4.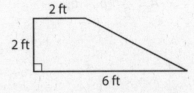

2 ft
2 ft
6 ft

_____

Find the area of each rhombus.

5.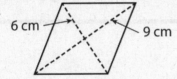

6 cm
9 cm

_____

6.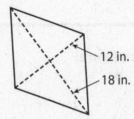

12 in.
18 in.

_____

Solve.

7. A desktop in the shape of a parallelogram has a base of 30 inches and a height of 40 inches. What is the area of the desktop?

_____

8. A rhombus has one diagonal that is 14 centimeters long and one diagonal that is 12 centimeters long. What is the area of the rhombus?

_____

9. The bases of a trapezoid are 24 feet and 16 feet. The height of the trapezoid is 12 feet. What is the area of the trapezoid?

_____

LESSON
13-1

Area of Quadrilaterals

Reteach

You can use formulas to find the areas of quadrilaterals.

The area A of a **parallelogram** is the product of its base b and its height h.

$$A = bh$$

$A = bh$
$\quad = 3 \cdot 7$
$\quad = 21 \text{ cm}^2$

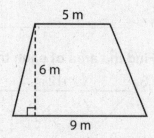

The area of a **trapezoid** is half its height multiplied by the sum of the lengths of its two bases.

$$A = \frac{1}{2}h(b_1 + b_2)$$

$A = \frac{1}{2}h(b_1 + b_2)$
$\quad = \frac{1}{2} \cdot 6(5 + 9)$
$\quad = \frac{1}{2} \cdot 6(14)$
$\quad = 3 \cdot 14$
$\quad = 42 \text{ m}^2$

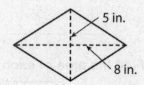

The area of a **rhombus** is half of the product of its two diagonals.

$$A = \frac{1}{2}d_1d_2$$

$A = \frac{1}{2}d_1d_2$
$\quad = \frac{1}{2}(5)(8)$
$\quad = 20 \text{ in.}^2$

Find the area of each figure.

1.

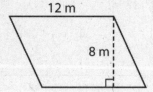

2.

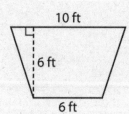

3.

4.

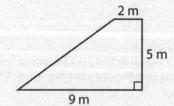

_____   _____

LESSON 13-2

Area of Triangles
Practice and Problem Solving: A/B

Find the area of each triangle.

1.

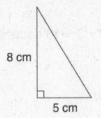

8 cm

5 cm

_____

2.

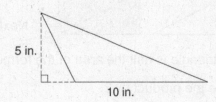

5 in.

10 in.

_____

3.

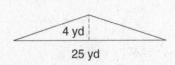

4 yd

25 yd

_____

4.

4 ft

3.5 ft

_____

Solve.

5. The front part of a tent is 8 feet long and 5 feet tall. What is the area of the front part of the tent?

_____

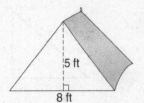

5 ft

8 ft

6. Kathy is playing a board game. The game pieces are each in the shape of a triangle. Each triangle has a base of 1.5 inches and a height of 2 inches. What is the area of a game piece?

_____

7. A triangular-shaped window has a base of 3 feet and a height of 4 feet. What is the area of the window?

_____

8. Landon has a triangular piece of paper. The base of the paper is $6\frac{1}{2}$ inches. The height of the paper is 8 inches. What is the area of the piece of paper?

_____

Name _____   Date _____ Class_____

LESSON
13-2

Area of Triangles

Reteach

To find the area of a triangle, first turn your triangle into a rectangle.

Next, find the area of the rectangle. $6 \cdot 3 = 18$ square units

The triangle is half the area of the formed rectangle or $A = \dfrac{1}{2} bh$, so

divide the product by 2.

$18 \div 2 = 9$ So, the area of the triangle is 9 square units.

Find the area of each triangle.

1.

4 cm
6 cm

2.

3 ft
4 ft

_____

3.

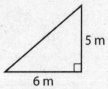
5 m
6 m

4.

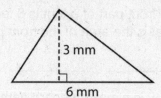
3 mm
6 mm

_____

5.

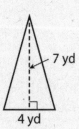
7 yd
4 yd

6.

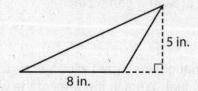
5 in.
8 in.

_____

LESSON 13-3

Solving Area Equations

Practice and Problem Solving: A/B

Solve.

1. The front of an A-frame house is in the shape of a triangle. The height of the house is 20 feet. The area of the front of the A-frame is 600 square feet. Write and solve an equation to find the base of the A-frame house.

   _____

2. A countertop is in the shape of a trapezoid. The lengths of the bases are $70\frac{1}{2}$ and $65\frac{1}{2}$ inches long. The area of the countertop is 1,224 square inches. Write and solve an equation to find the height of the countertop.

   _____

3. The top of a coffee table is in the shape of a rectangle. The length of the top of the coffee table is 3.5 feet and the area is 10.5 square feet. What is the width of the top of the coffee table?

   _____

4. Jacob made a banner for a sporting event in the shape of a parallelogram. The area of the banner is $127\frac{1}{2}$ square centimeters. The height of the banner is $4\frac{1}{4}$ centimeters. What is the base of the banner?

   _____

5. McKenzie has enough paint to paint 108 square feet. She wants to paint her garage door, which has a height of 12 feet. The garage door is in the shape of a rectangle. If McKenzie has just enough paint to cover the garage door, what is the width of the door?

   _____

LESSON 13-3

Solving Area Equations

Reteach

You can use area formulas to find missing dimensions in figures.

The formula for area of a parallelogram is $A = bh$.

The formula for area of a trapezoid is $A = \frac{1}{2}h(b_1 + b_2)$.

The formula for area of a rhombus is $A = \frac{1}{2}d_1d_2$.

The formula for area of a triangle is $A = \frac{1}{2}bh$.

Suppose you know the area of a triangle is 28 square feet. You also know the length of the base of the triangle is 7 feet. What is the height of the triangle?

Use the formula for area of a triangle. $A = \frac{1}{2}bh$

Substitute known values. $28 = \frac{1}{2}(7)h$

Multiply both sides by 2. $56 = 7h$

Divide both sides by 7. $8 = h$

The height of the triangle is 8 feet.

Solve.

1. The area of a parallelogram is 150 square meters. The height of the parallelogram is 15 meters. What is the length of the parallelogram?

_____

2. The length of one diagonal of a rhombus is 8 cm. The area of the rhombus is 72 square centimeters. What is the length of the other diagonal of the rhombus?

_____

3. The area of a triangle is 32 square inches. The height of the triangle is 8 inches. What is the length of the base of the triangle?

_____

4. The area of a rectangle is 34 square yards. The length of the rectangle is 17 yards. What is the width of the rectangle?

_____

5. The area of a trapezoid is 39 square millimeters. The height of the trapezoid is 6 millimeters. One of the base lengths of the trapezoid is 5 millimeters. What is the length of the other base of the trapezoid?

_____

LESSON 13-4

Area of Polygons

Practice and Problem Solving: A/B

Find the area of each polygon.

1.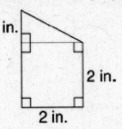

2.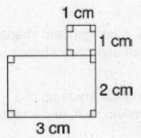

_____

3.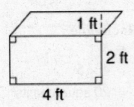

4.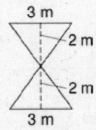

_____

5.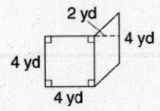

6.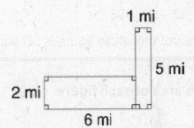

_____

Solve.

7. The shape of Nevada can almost be divided into a perfect rectangle and a perfect triangle. About how many square miles does Nevada cover?

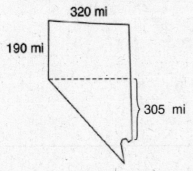

8. The shape of Oklahoma can almost be divided into 2 perfect rectangles and 1 triangle. About how many square miles does Oklahoma cover?

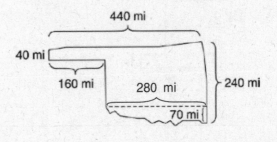

_____

LESSON 13-4

Area of Polygons
Reteach

Sometimes you can use area formulas you know to help you find the area of more complex figures.

You can break a polygon into shapes that you know. Then use those shapes to find the area.

The figure at right is made up of a triangle, a parallelogram, and a rectangle.

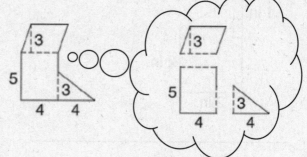

Triangle

$A = \dfrac{1}{2}bh$

$= \dfrac{1}{2}(3 \times 4)$

$= 6$ square units

Parallelogram

$A = bh$

$= 3 \times 4$

$= 12$ square units

Rectangle

$A = lw$

$= 4 \times 5$

$= 20$ square units

Finally, find the sum of all three areas.

$6 + 12 + 20 = 38$

The area of the whole figure is 38 square units.

Find the area of each figure.

1.

_____

2.

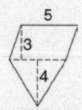

_____

3.

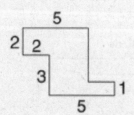

_____

4.

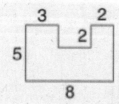

_____

LESSON
14-1

Distance in the Coordinate Plane

Practice and Problem Solving: A/B

Name the coordinates of each reflection.

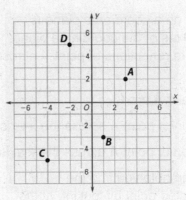

1. Point *A* across the *x*-axis

   New point: (_____, _____)

2. Point *B* across the *y*-axis

   New point: (_____, _____)

3. Point *C* across the *x*-axis

   New point: (_____, _____)

4. Point *D* across the *y*-axis

   New point: (_____, _____)

Name the coordinates of each reflection of the given point.

5. $M(-2, -6)$

   Across the *y*-axis: (_____, _____)

   Across the *x*-axis: (_____, _____)

6. $N(4, 1)$

   Across the *x*-axis: (_____, _____)

   Across the *y*-axis: (_____, _____)

Find the distance between the points.

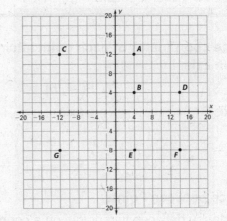

7. *A* and *B*: _____

8. *A* and *C*: _____

9. *B* and *D*: _____

10. *C* and *G*: _____

11. *D* and *F*: _____

12. *E* and *F*: _____

13. *E* and *B*: _____

14. *E* and *A*: _____

15. *E* and *G*: _____

16. *F* and *G*: _____

Solve.

17. A taxi travels 25 kilometers east of an airport. Then, it travels from that
    point to a point that is 40 kilometers west of the airport. Finally, the taxi
    returns to the airport. How far did the taxi travel? Show your work.

_____

LESSON 14-1

Distance in the Coordinate Plane
Reteach

Reflecting a Point

In this lesson, a point on a coordinate plane is reflected across the axes of the coordinate plane. The points *B* and *C* are reflections of point *A* across the *x*- and *y*-axes.

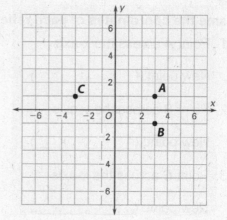

The coordinates of point *A* are (3, 1).

Point *B* is the reflection of point *A* across the *x*-axis.

Point *C* is the reflection of point *A* across the *y*-axis.

The following rules can help you find the coordinates of a reflected point by looking at the signs of the coordinates.

Reflecting across the *x*-axis

"Reflect across *x*. ⟶ Change the *y*."

In this example, point *A*'s *x*-coordinate, +3, stays the same when point *A* is reflected across the *x*-axis to become point *B*. Point *A*'s *y*-coordinate, +1, switches to –1 to become point *B*.
So, point *B*'s coordinates are (3, –1).

Reflecting across the *y*-axis

"Reflect across *y*. ⟶ Change the *x*."

In this example, point *A*'s *y*-coordinate, +1, stays the same when point *A* is reflected across the *y*-axis to become point *C*. Point *A*'s *x*-coordinate, +3, switches to –3 to become point *C*.
So, point *C*'s coordinates are (–3, 1).

Name the coordinates of each point after it is reflected across the given axis.

1. *A*(1, 3)

   x-axis

   (____, ____)

2. *B*(–4, 5)

   y-axis

   (____, ____)

3. *C*(6, –7)

   y-axis

   (____, ____)

4. *D*(–8, –9)

   x-axis

   (____, ____)

Distance between Points

The distance between two points on a coordinate plane depends on whether their *x*- or *y*-coordinates are different. Look at the points on the grid above to solve the problems.

The distance between points *A* and *B* is the absolute value of the difference of the *y*-coordinates of the points.

The distance between points *A* and *C* is the absolute value of the difference of the *x*-coordinates of the points.

Find the distance between the two points.

5. points *A* and *B*

   _____ units

6. points *A* and *C*

   _____ units

LESSON 14-2

Polygons in the Coordinate Plane

Practice and Problem Solving: A/B

List all of the polygons that can be formed by using some or all of the lettered vertices shown in the coordinate plane.

1. _____

   _____

   _____

   _____

   _____

   _____

   _____

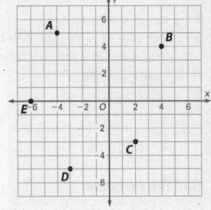

Tell how many polygons can be formed by each set of points or set of points and a line.

2. (0, 1) and (2, 3)

3. (4, 5), (6, 7), and (8, 9)

4. (3, 5) and the *x*-axis.

_____   _____   _____

Find the perimeter and area of each polygon. Show your work.

5.

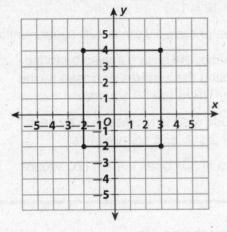

6.

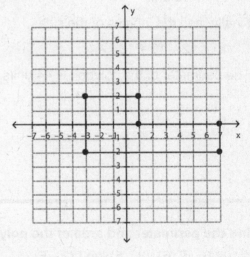

Perimeter: _____   Perimeter: _____

_____   _____

Area: _____   Area: _____

_____   _____

LESSON 14-2

Polygons in the Coordinate Plane
Reteach

Polygons are formed from three or more points, called *vertices*, that are connected by line segments and that enclose an area.

If the lengths of the sides are known, the area and perimeter of a polygon can be found. They can also be found if the coordinates of the vertices are known.

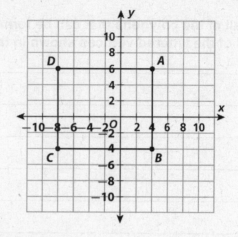

Find the Perimeter

First, identify the coordinates of the points that form the vertices of the polygon.

A: (4, 6); B: (4, –4); C: (–8, –4); D: (–8, 6)

Next, find the lengths of the sides.

AB = 10 units

BC = 12 units

CD = 10 units

DA = 12 units

Finally, add the lengths of the sides.

10 + 12 + 10 + 12 = 44

The perimeter of the polygon is 44 units.

Find the Area

First, identify the polygon. The figure is a rectangle, so its area is the product of its length and width.

Next, use the coordinates of the points to find the length and width.

AB = 10 units

BC = 12 units

Finally, multiply the length and width.

10 × 12 = 120

The area of the polygon is 120 square units.

In this case, the area can also be found by counting the squares enclosed by the polygon. There are 30 squares.

How much area is represented by each square? 2 × 2, or 4 square units.

The area is 30 cubes × 4, or 120 square units.

Find the perimeter and area of the polygon enclosed by the points.

1. (8, 6), (2, 6), (8, –5), and (2, –5)

   Side lengths: _____

   Perimeter: _____

   Area: _____

2. (0, 0), (0, 7), (7, 7), and (7, 0)

   Side lengths: _____

   Perimeter: _____

   Area: _____

LESSON 15-1

Nets and Surface Area

Practice and Problem Solving: A/B

Find the surface area of each net.

1. Each square is one square meter.

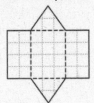

_____ square meters

2. Each square is one square yard

_____ square yards

3. A square pyramid has _____ square base

and _____ triangular faces.

Find its surface area.

a. The area of the base is _____ square centimeters.

b. The area of the four faces is _____ square centimeters.

c. The surface area is _____ square centimeters.

4. Josef makes wooden boxes for jewelry. He made 5 boxes like the one shown, and wants to cover all the outside faces with fabric.

a. Find the surface area of one box.

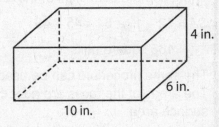

_____

b. Find the total surface area of 5 boxes.

_____

c. The fabric Josef is using comes in 100 square-inch pieces that cost $6.25 each. What will his fabric cost?

_____

Calculate the surface area for each figure.

5. The base is a square.

7.8 m

6.4 m

Surface area:

6.

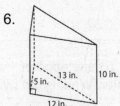

Surface area:

_____   _____

LESSON 15-1 Nets and Surface Area
Reteach

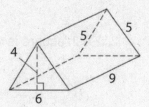

To find the surface area of the regular triangular prism above, first find the area of each face or base.

2 congruent triangular bases   3 rectangular faces

$h = 4$
$b = 6$

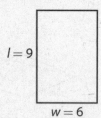 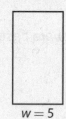 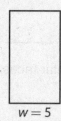

$l = 9$

$w = 6$ $w = 5$ $w = 5$

$A = \frac{1}{2}bh$ $A = lw$ $A = lw$

$= \frac{1}{2}(6 \cdot 4)$ $= (9 \cdot 6)$ $= (9 \cdot 5)$

$= 12$ square units $= 54$ $= 45$

Then, find the sum of all of the faces of the prism.

$SA = 12 + 12 + 54 + 45 + 45$

$\quad = 168$ square units

The same procedure can be used to find the surface area of a **pyramid**. The areas of the faces are added to the area of the base to give the total surface area.

Solve each problem.

1. A prism has isosceles triangle bases with leg lengths of 5 inches, 5 inches, and 8 inches, and a height of 3 inches. The distance between the bases is 12 inches. Find the surface area. Show your work.

_____

2. A square pyramid has a base edge of 1 meter. The height of each triangular face is 1 meter. What is the pyramid's surface area? Show your work.

_____

LESSON 15-2

Volume of Rectangular Prisms

Practice and Problem Solving: A/B

Use the formula for the volume of a rectangular solid to find the volume of each solid in cubic meters.

1.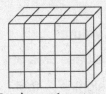

   5 cubes =1 meter

   Length:

   _____ cubes = _____ meter

   Width:

   _____ cubes = _____ meter

   Height:

   _____ cubes = _____ meter

   Volume: _____

2.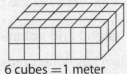

   6 cubes =1 meter

   Length:

   _____ cubes = _____ meter

   Width:

   _____ cubes = _____ meter

   Height:

   _____ cubes = _____ meter

   Volume: _____

Solve.

3. A student made a toy chest for his baby sister's square building blocks.
   Six layers of blocks can fit in the box, and each layer has 15 blocks.
   How many building blocks can the toy chest hold? Show your work.

   _____

Find the volume of each figure. Show your work. Simplify your answers.

4. 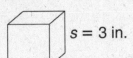 $s = 3$ in.

5.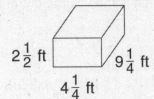

   $2\frac{1}{2}$ ft $9\frac{1}{4}$ ft

   $4\frac{1}{4}$ ft

6.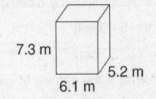

   7.3 m

   6.1 m   5.2 m

   _____   _____   _____

   _____   _____   _____

LESSON 15-2 Volume of Rectangular Prisms
Reteach

The volume of a rectangular prism is found by multiplying its length, width, and height. In some cases, instead of the length and width, the area of one of the bases of the prism will be known.

Length, width, height, and volume

A rectangular prism has dimensions of 2.5 meters, 4.3 meters, and 5.1 meters. What is its volume to two significant figures?

Solution

$V = l \times w \times h$

$V = 2.5 \times 4.3 \times 5.1$

$\quad = 54.825$

To two significant figures, the volume of the prism is 55 cubic meters.

Base area, height, and volume

A rectangular prism has a base area of $\frac{2}{3}$ of a square foot. Its height is $\frac{1}{2}$ foot. What is its volume?

Solution

$V = A_{base} \times h$

$V = \frac{2}{3} \times \frac{1}{2} = \frac{1}{3}$

The volume of the prism is $\frac{1}{3}$ cubic foot.

Find the volume of a rectangular prism with the given dimensions.

1. length: $\frac{2}{3}$ yd; width: $\frac{5}{6}$ yd; height: $\frac{4}{5}$ yd _____

2. base area: 12.5 m²; height: 1.2 m _____

The density of a metal in a sample is the mass of the sample divided by the volume of the sample. The units are mass per unit volume.

Problem The mass of a sample of metal is 2,800 grams. The sample is in the shape of a rectangular prism that measures 5 centimeters by 7 centimeters by 8 centimeters. What is the volume of the sample?

$V = 5 \times 7 \times 8$

$\quad = 280 \text{ cm}^3$

What is the density of the sample?

$2,800 \div 280 = 10 \text{ g/cm}^3$

---

3. A sample of metal has a mass of 3,600 grams. The sample is in the shape of a rectangular prism that has dimensions of 2 centimeters by 3 centimeters by 4 centimeters. What is the density of the sample?

_____

LESSON
15-3

Solving Volume Equations
Practice and Problem Solving: A/B

Find the volume of each figure.

1.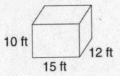
10 ft
12 ft
15 ft

_____

2.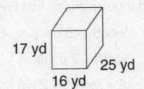
17 yd
25 yd
16 yd

_____

3.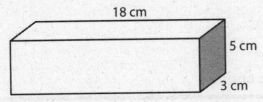
18 cm
5 cm
3 cm

_____

4.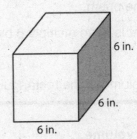
6 in.
6 in.
6 in.

_____

Solve.

5. Fawn built a sandbox that is 6 feet long, 5 feet wide, and $\frac{1}{2}$ foot tall.

   How many cubic feet of sand does she need to fill the box?

   _____

6. A pack of gum is in the shape of a rectangular prism with a length of
   8 centimeters and width of 2 centimeters. The volume of the pack of
   gum is 48 cubic centimeters. What is the height of the pack of gum?

   _____

7. A block of cheese is in the shape of a rectangular prism with a width of
   2.5 inches and a height of 5 inches. The volume of the block of cheese
   is 75 cubic inches. What is the length of the block of cheese?

   _____

8. A tissue box is in the shape of a rectangular prism with an area of
   528 cubic inches. The length of the box of tissues is 12 inches and the

   height is $5\frac{1}{2}$ inches. What is the width of the box of tissues?

   _____

Solving Volume Equations
Reteach

Volume is the number of cubic units needed to fill a space. To find the volume of a rectangular prism, first find the area of the base.

length = 3 units

width = 2 units

$A = lw = 3 \cdot 2 = 6$ square units

The area of the base tells you how many cubic units are in the first layer of the prism.

The height is 4, so multiply 6 by 4.

$6 \cdot 4 = 24$

So, the volume of the rectangular prism is 24 cubic units.

Find each volume.

1.

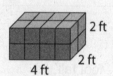

2 ft
2 ft
4 ft

_____

2.

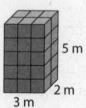

5 m
2 m
3 m

_____

3.

15 cm
3 cm
2 cm

_____

4.

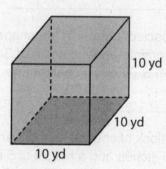

10 yd
10 yd
10 yd

_____

5.

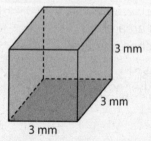

3 mm
3 mm
3 mm

_____

6.

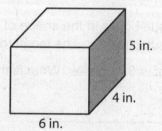

5 in.
4 in.
6 in.

_____

Measures of Center

Practice and Problem Solving: A/B

LESSON 16-1

Use the situation below to complete Exercises 1–4.

The heights (in inches) of the starting players on a high school basketball team are as follows: 72, 75, 78, 72, 73.

1. How many starting players are there? _____

2. What is the mean height? _____

3. What is the median height? _____

4. Does one measure describe the data better than the other? Explain.

_____

_____

In Exercises 5–7, find the mean and median of each data set.

5. Daily high temperatures (°F): 45, 50, 47, 52, 53, 45, 51

   Mean: _____ Median: _____

6. Brian's math test scores: 86, 90, 93, 85, 79, 92

   Mean: _____ Median: _____

7. Players' heart rates (beats per minute): 70, 68, 70, 72, 68, 66, 65, 73

   Mean: _____ Median: _____

8. Hikers spent the following amounts of time (in minutes) to complete a nature hike: 48, 46, 52, 57, 58, 52, 61, 56.

   a. Find the mean and median times.

   Mean: _____ Median: _____

   b. Does one measure describe the data better than the other? Explain.

   _____

   c. Suppose another hiker takes 92 minutes to complete the hike. Find the mean and median times including this new time.

   Mean: _____ Median: _____

   d. Does one measure describe the data better than the other now? Explain.

   _____

   _____

Measures of Center
Reteach

When calculating the mean, you can use *compatible numbers* to find the sum of the data values. Compatible numbers make calculations easier. For example, adding multiples of 5 or 10 is easier than adding all of the individual data values.

A group of students are asked how many hours they spend watching television during one week. Their responses are: 15, 7, 12, 8, 4, 13, 11. What is the mean?

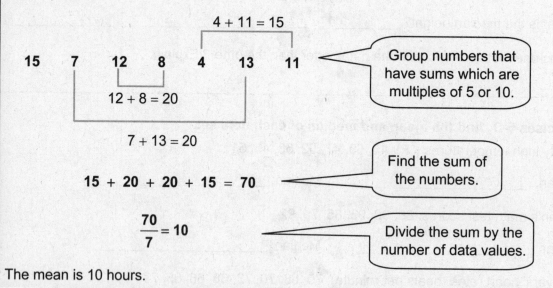

$$4 + 11 = 15$$

15   7   12   8   4   13   11

Group numbers that have sums which are multiples of 5 or 10.

$$12 + 8 = 20$$

$$7 + 13 = 20$$

$$15 + 20 + 20 + 15 = 70$$

Find the sum of the numbers.

$$\frac{70}{7} = 10$$

Divide the sum by the number of data values.

The mean is 10 hours.

Use compatible numbers to find the mean.

1. The costs (in dollars) of items on a lunch menu are 9, 14, 11, 6, 16, 10.

   Mean: _____

2. The numbers of students in Mr. Silva's math classes are 19, 18, 22, 24, 20, 18, 26.

   Mean: _____

3. In the television viewing data above, is there more than one way to pair the data values to form compatible numbers? Explain.

   _____

   _____

LESSON 16-2

Mean Absolute Deviation

Practice and Problem Solving: A/B

Find the *mean absolute deviation* for each data set.

1. The number of kittens in 10 litters: 4, 5, 5, 6, 6, 7, 8, 8, 8, and 9

   _____

2. The number of approved soy-based containers produced in 10 stamping runs of 240 containers: 225, 227, 227, 228, 230, 230, 231, 238, 238, and 240

   _____

3. Two bowlers bowl the following number of strikes in 9 games.

1ˢᵗ **bowler**	8	5	5	6	8	7	4	7	6
2ⁿᵈ **bowler**	10	6	8	8	5	5	6	8	9

   What is the mean and the mean absolute deviation of the number of strikes of each bowler?

   _____

   _____

   What does the mean absolute deviation suggest about each bowler's consistency?

   _____

   _____

Use a spreadsheet program to complete the problem.

4. A tool manufacturer machines an 8-centimeter brass-alloy spindle for one of its tools. The first table shows the variation in thousandths of a centimeter in nine of the spindles.

A2				f_x					
	A	B	C	D	E	F	G	H	I	J
1	8.002	8.002	8	7.997	8.004	7.999	8.002	8.001	7.997	
2										
3										
4										

   Complete the spreadsheet as shown to find the mean spindle length.

DATE			× ✓ f_x	=AVERAGE(A1:I1)					
	A	B	C	D	E	F	G	H	I	J
1	8.002	8.002	8	7.997	8.004	7.999	8.002	8.001	7.997	
2	mean =	=AVERAGE(A1:I1)								
3										

   Mean: _____

5. Use the spreadsheet to find the mean absolute deviation of the spindle lengths.

DATE			× ✓ f_x	=AVEDEV(A1:I1)					
	A	B	C	D	E	F	G	H	I	J
1	8.002	8.002	8	7.997	8.004	7.999	8.002	8.001	7.997	
2	mean =									
3	MAD =	=AVEDEV(A1:I1)								
4										

   MAD: _____

LESSON 16-2	# Mean Absolute Deviation

Reteach

The *mean absolute deviation*, or *MAD*, is the average of how far the elements in a data set are from the *mean* of the data set.

If you think of MAD as a distance, it will always be a positive number. For two or more comparable data sets, the larger the MAD is, the more "spread out" the elements of a data set are, such as in the example.

Example

Step 1 Find the mean.

The mean of these two data sets of the number of eggs in 10 nests of two birds of the same species over several breeding cycles:

- Bird *A*: 3, 3, 4, 2, 3, 4, 5, 1, 2, and 2
- Bird *B*: 1, 1, 3, 6, 2, 2, 3, 5, 4, and 1

For Bird *A*: mean = 29 ÷ 10 = 2.9 or about 3 eggs
For Bird *B*: mean = 28 ÷ 10 = 2.8 or about 3 eggs

Step 2 Find the mean absolute deviation. First, find the deviation of each element from the mean by subtracting the element's value from the mean or vice versa. This gives these deviations for the 10 elements in each data set.

Bird *A*: 0.1, 0.1, 1.1, 0.9, 0.1, 1.1, 2.1, 1.9, 0.9, and 0.9
Bird *B*: 1.8, 1.8, 0.2, 3.2, 0.8, 0.8, 0.2, 2.2, 1.2, and 1.8

Then add the deviations for each bird and divide by the number of breeding cycles.

For Bird *A*: MAD = 9.2 ÷ 10 = 0.92
For Bird *B*: MAD = 14 ÷ 10 = 1.4

In this example, the mean number of eggs in each bird's nest is almost the same. However, the mean absolute deviations, or MAD, of the two data sets are different. The number of eggs in Bird *B*'s nests over 10 breeding cycles show more **variability**, or the "number of eggs varied more" than did the number of eggs in Bird *A*'s nests over 10 cycles.

Notice that both MAD values round to one egg. What do you think will happen to these MAD values over a larger number of breeding cycles?

Find the mean absolute deviation by hand calculations or with a spreadsheet program.

1. Data:

   0.1, 0.15, 0.09, 0.11, and 0.13

   MAD: _____

2. Data:

   250, 249, 251, 253, and 253

   MAD: _____

LESSON
16-3

Box Plots

Practice and Problem Solving: A/B

High Temperatures						
69	73	72	66	64	64	61
70	78	78	74	69	61	62

The high temperatures for 2 weeks are shown at the right. Use the data set for Exercises 1–7.

1. Order the data from least to greatest.

   _____

2. Find the median. _____

3. Find the lower quartile. _____

4. Find the upper quartile. _____

5. Make a box plot for the data.

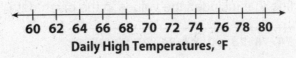

   Daily High Temperatures, °F

6. Find the IQR. _____   7. Find the range. _____

Use the situation and data given below to complete Exercises 8–10.

Two classes collected canned food for the local food bank. Below are the number of cans collected each week.

   Class A: 18 20 15 33 30 23 38 34 40 28 18 33

   Class B: 18 27 29 20 26 26 29 30 24 28 29 28

8. Arrange the data for each class in order from least to greatest.

   Class A: _____

   Class B: _____

9. Find the median, the range, and the IQR of each data set.

   Class A: median:_____   range:_____   IQR:_____

   Class B: median:_____   range:_____   IQR:_____

10. Compare and contrast the box plots for the two data sets.

   _____

   _____

LESSON 16-3
Box Plots
Reteach

A **box plot** gives you a visual display of how data are distributed.

Here are the scores Ed received on 9 quizzes: 76, 80, 89, 90, 70, 86, 87, 76, 80.

Step 1: List the scores in order from least to greatest.

Step 2: Identify the least and greatest values.

Step 3: Identify the median. If there is an odd number of values, the median is the middle value.

Step 4: Identify the lower quartile and upper quartile. If there is an even number of values above or below the median, the lower or upper quartile is the average of the two middle values.

Step 5: Draw a number line that includes the values in the given data.

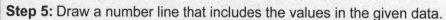
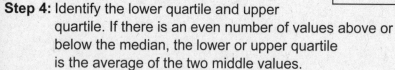

Step 6: Place dots above the number lines at each value you identified in Steps 2–4. Draw a box starting at the lower quartile and ending at the upper quartile. Mark the median, too.

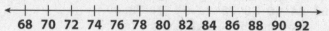
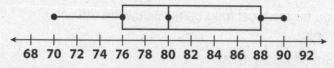

Use the data at the right for Exercises 1–5. Complete each statement.

20	6	15
10	14	15
8	10	12

1. List the data in order: _____

2. Least value: _____ Greatest value: _____

3. Median: _____

4. Lower quartile: _____ Upper quartile: _____

5. Draw a box plot for the data.

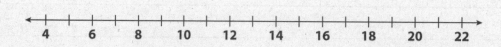

LESSON 16-4

Dot Plots and Data Distribution

Practice and Problem Solving: A/B

Tell whether each question is a statistical question. If it is a statistical question, identify the units for the answer.

1. How far do you travel to get to school? _____

2. How tall is the door to this classroom? _____

Use the data set at the right and the description below to complete Exercises 3–6.

The class took a survey about how many people live in each student's home. The results are shown at the right.

People in Our Homes
4, 2, 5, 4, 2, 6, 4, 3, 4, 3, 5, 6,
2, 7, 3, 2, 5, 3, 4,11, 4, 5, 3

3. Make a dot plot of the data.

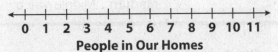

People in Our Homes

4. Find the mean, median, and range of the data.

mean:_____; median:_____; range:_____

5. Describe the spread, center, and shape of the data distribution.

_____

_____

6. Which number is an outlier in the data set? Explain what effect the outlier has on the measures of center and spread.

_____

_____

7. Survey 12 students to find how many people live in their homes. Record the data below. Make a box plot at the right.

_____

_____

LESSON 16-4

Dot Plots and Data Distribution
Reteach

A **dot plot** gives you a visual display of how data are distributed.

Example: Here are the scores Yolanda received on math quizzes: 6, 10, 9, 9, 10, 8, 7, 7, and 10. <u>Make a dot plot for Yolanda's quiz scores.</u>

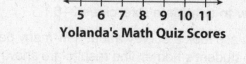

Yolanda's Math Quiz Scores

Step 1: Draw a number line.

Step 2: Write the title below the number line.

Step 3: For each number in the data set, put a dot above that number on the number line.

Yolanda's Math Quiz Scores

<u>Describe the dot plot by identifying the **range**, the **mean,** and the **median.**</u>

Step 4: Identify the range. $10 - 6 = 4$

Step 5: Find the mean. $76 \div 9 = 8.4$

Step 6: Find the median. 9

Range: Greatest value − least value

Mean: $\dfrac{\text{Sum of data values}}{\text{Number of data values}}$

Median: Middle value

Use the data set at the right to complete Exercises 1–4.

1. Draw a dot plot for the data.

Game Scores			
12	6	15	10
14	15	8	10
12	21	15	8

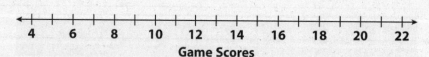

Game Scores

2. Find the range. _____

3. Find the mean. _____

4. Find the median. _____

LESSON
16-5

Histograms

Practice and Problem Solving: A/B

**Use the data in the chart and the description
below to complete Exercises 1–2.**

The data set lists the heights of the Houston Rockets players during the
2011–2012 basketball season.

Players' Heights
81 80 79 72 72 78 82
80 80 76 87 65 79 82
80 79 81 71 77

1. Complete the frequency table.
   Use an interval of 5.

Players' Heights	
Heights (in.)	**Frequency**
65–69	

2. Complete the histogram.

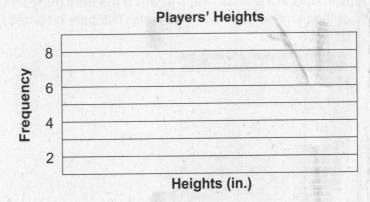

Solve. Use the histogram or the set of data. Tell which you used.

3. Find the range, the median, and the mean of the players' heights.

   a. range   b. median   c. mode

   _____   _____   _____

4. Based on this data, what do you think is the average height of players
   in the National Basketball Association? Explain how you decided on
   your answer including which display of data you used.

   _____

   _____

   _____

LESSON 16-5 Histograms
Reteach

Histograms can be used to display data. Use intervals of 10.

Pounds of Newspapers Collected for Recycling				
12	28	24	32	35
31	38	55	43	52
42	49	18	22	15
47	37	19	31	37

Pounds of Newspapers

Interval	Frequency
1–10	0
11–20	4
21–30	3
31–40	7
41–50	4
51–60	2

A **histogram** is a bar graph in which the bars represent the frequencies of the numeric data within intervals. The bars on a histogram touch, but do not overlap.

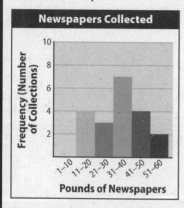

Use the histogram to complete Exercises 1–4.

1. Which interval has the greatest number of collections?

    _____

    _____

2. Were there any collections of less than 11 pounds? Explain your answer.

    _____

    _____

3. Which display can you use to find the median? _____

4. What is the median of the data? _____